Library of
Davidson College

Punishing International Terrorists

Punishing International Terrorists

The Legal Framework for Policy Initiatives

John F. Murphy
Villanova University

ROWMAN & ALLANHELD
PUBLISHERS

ROWMAN & ALLANHELD

Published in the United States of America in 1985
by Rowman & Allanheld, Publishers
(a division of Littlefield, Adams & Company)
81 Adams Drive, Totowa, New Jersey 07512

Copyright © 1985 by Rowman & Allanheld

All rights reserved. No part of this publication
may be reproduced, stored in a retrieval system, or
transmitted in any form or by any means, electronic,
mechanical, photocopying, recording, or otherwise,
without the prior permission of the publisher.

Library of Congress Cataloging-in-Publication Data

Murphy, John Francis, 1937–
  Punishing international terrorists.

  Includes bibliographies and index.
  1. Terrorism. I. Title.
JX5420.M88   1985   364.1   85-15845
ISBN 0-8476-7449-5

85 86 87 / 10 9 8 7 6 5 4 3 2 1
Printed in the United States of America

Contents

Tables	vii
Acknowledgments	ix
Introduction: Overview and Background	1
Terrorism: The Definitional Focus, *3*	

PART ONE: APPREHENSION, PROSECUTION, AND PUNISHMENT OF TERRORISTS: THE LEGAL FRAMEWORK

1 Counterterrorist Conventions — *Aut Dedere, Aut Judicare* — 9
Global Conventions, *9;* Regional Conventions, *11;* Bilateral Agreements, *16;* Sanctions Against the Harboring of Hijackers, *17;* Implementation: National Legislation and Court Decisions, *21;* Notes, *32*

2 Extradition — 36
Regional Arrangements, *37;* Bilateral Extradition Agreements: The Traditional Model, *42;* The Political Offense Exception and International Terrorism, *45;* Recent Developments Regarding Extradition, the Political Offense Exception, and International Terrorism, *56;* Notes, *77*

3 Methods of Rendition Other Than Extradition — 81
Exclusion and Deportation, *81;* Illegal Methods of Rendition: Abduction and Unlawful Seizure, *89;* Notes, *93*

4 International Judicial Assistance in Criminal Matters — 95
United States Law and Experience, *96;* The Western European Experience: A Glance at Austria, *100;* Notes, *102*

PART TWO: PUNISHING INTERNATIONAL TERRORISTS: THE ELUSIVE GOAL

5 **Apprehension, Prosecution, and Punishment of International Terrorists: State Practice**   107
  Attacks Against Aircraft and Aviation Facilities, *108;*
  Other Manifestations of Terrorist Activity, *116*; Notes, *122*

6 **Conclusions and Recommendations**   124
  Extradition—United States Law and Practice, *124;*
  Extradition—International Initiatives, *129;* Exclusion and Deportation, *130;* Prosecution, Punishment, and the Protection of Fundamental Human Rights, *131;*
  International Judicial Assistance in Criminal Matters, *133;*
  A Brief Word on the Problem of Safe-Haven States, *134;*
  Notes, *135*

Index   137

Tables

5.1 Domestic and Foreign Aircraft Hijackings, 1977–1982   110

5.2 International Rendition of Hijackers, 1977–1981   113

5.3 Persons Involved in the Seventy-Two Hijackings
     of U.S.-Registered Aircraft, 1977–1982   114

5.4 Summary of Hijackings, 1977–1982   115

Acknowledgments

A number of people have been very helpful to me in writing this monograph. I want to acknowledge their assistance, on the understanding that the views expressed in this study are solely my own.

Michael Abbell, formerly Associate Director, Office of International Affairs, Criminal Division, Department of Justice, and now in private practice in Washington, D.C., has been especially generous of his time and expertise. The same is true of James Busuttil, formerly of the Legal Adviser's Office, Department of State, and now in private practice in New York; Terrell E. Arnold, formerly Principal Deputy Director, Office of Counter-Terrorism and Emergency Planning, Department of State; and Ambassador Robert M. Sayre, formerly Director, Office for Counter-Terrorism and Emergency Planning.

Virgil L. (Bud) Krohn, Special Assistant for Intelligence, Office of Civil Aviation Security, Federal Aviation Administration, very kindly provided me with substantial data regarding terrorist attacks on civil aviation; and Richard Hayes, Dewey Covington, and Miriam Steiner of Defense Systems, Inc., McClean, Virginia, did the same with regard to other kinds of terrorist activity. The Federal Bureau of Investigation supplied me with data regarding terrorist activity in the United States.

M. Cherif Bassiouni, Professor of Law at DePaul University and an outstanding authority on international extradition, helped to inform me on the use of various methods of rendition of international terrorists. Alfred P. Rubin, Professor of International Law, Fletcher School of Law and Diplomacy and Chairman of the International Law Association's Committee on International Terrorism, whose reports are highlighted in this study, kept me informed of the committee's proceedings. Waldemar Solf, Chairman of the American Bar Association's International Criminal Law Committee, similarly kept me informed of that committee's work.

Marguerite Trossevin, my research assistant for the 1983-1984 academic year, provided invaluable assistance, including the drafting of the tables in Part II of the study. Maryfrances Metrick, my reference assistant for 1984-1985, provided assistance in research, proofreading, and chapter note form checking.

Joan DeLong and Terri LaVerghetta of the Villanova Law School secreterial staff typed innumerable drafts of this study with patience and skill.

Last but not least I wish to express my thanks to John Norton Moore, Walter L. Brown Professor of Law at the University of Virginia and Chairman, The American Bar Association's Standing Committee on Law and National Security, for his support and guidance in completing this study. Thanks are also due to the Standing Committee for its permission to publish the study. Responsibility for the views expressed in the study, however, is solely my own.

John F. Murphy
Villanova, Pennsylvania
September 30, 1985

Introduction:
Overview and Background

In attempting to combat terrorist activities, government officials may take action at three different stages of possible involvement. The first, and ideal stage, is before the terrorist act occurs. That is, steps may be taken to prevent the terrorist activity, through, for example, security devices at airports; guards at nuclear plants or at critical "nodes" of energy sources; effective intelligence operations that result in apprehension of the terrorist at the initiation stage of his activities; and general educational efforts designed to minimize public support for terrorist activities. If these steps fail, then government officials may be forced to manage a terrorist incident in progress. This may involve such techniques as negotiations with terrorists who have occupied an embassy, hijacked a plane, or commandeered a train. It may involve public health measures to minimize damage caused by a terrorist bomb explosion, or efforts to use the media and other sources of communication to prevent public panic (for example, if a nuclear explosion were threatened). Finally, if the terrorist act is successfully completed, and the terrorist escapes the scene of his crime, the law enforcement effort is to apprehend, prosecute, and, if convicted, punish him. This third stage is the focus of this study.

A basic and preliminary question which must be addressed is whether the apprehension, prosecution, and punishment of terrorists is an effective measure for combating terrorism. As Professor Bassiouni has pointed out, the terrorist, by definition, is an ideologically motivated offender who rejects the legal characterization of his acts as criminal and who may regard the prospect of a prison term as a small price to pay for furthering his cause.[1] Indeed, as the deaths through voluntary starvation of the Irish Republican Army (IRA) terrorists demonstrate, prison may be an environment in which further sacrifices for the cause are undertaken.

To be sure, a prison term serves the minimal purpose of taking the terrorist off the street and preventing his engaging in further violence against society. But his presence in jail may stimulate further terrorist activities by his colleagues with a view to forcing his release. The taking of hostages has been an especially effective tactic to this end.

One should not conclude, however, that because the hard-core terrorist is unlikely to be deterred by the prospect of punishment, the prosecution and punishment of terrorists plays no useful role in deterring terrorism. Legal proscriptions against terrorism, at both the national and international levels, serve at a minimum to support the premise that terrorism is a criminal activity unjustified by the particular cause the terrorist espouses. Codification of humanitarian values into legal instruments, especially if accompanied by educational efforts, may be a helpful tactic in "ideological warfare" against terrorism.[2] Enforcement of the law and values reflected in these legal instruments is a crucial step to ensure their continued viability.

This study is not concerned with national terrorism—that is, terrorist actions that occur entirely within the boundaries of a single country. Nor is it concerned with the variant of national terrorism sometimes called "transnational terrorism," where the victim of an attack in a particular country is a foreign national (for example, a diplomat or an executive of a transnational corporation). Rather, this study is concerned only with the type of "international terrorism" where the terrorist commits his act in one country, flees, and is apprehended in another country. Upon apprehension, the issue arises as to whether the terrorist is to be prosecuted and, if so, where. In other words, is the terrorist to be returned to the country where he allegedly committed his crime and which seeks his return (hereinafter the "requesting country"), or should he be prosecuted instead in the country where he was apprehended (hereinafter "requested country")? If he is to be prosecuted in the requested country, will the prosecutorial authorities there be able to obtain the evidence necessary to convict him through international judicial assistance in criminal matters? Finally, are there certain situations where the alleged terrorist should be let free, despite evidence that he may have committed serious crimes? If so, what are these situations?

The primary goal of any civilized criminal process is to punish terrorists for their crimes in a manner consistent with the protection of the fundamental rights of the accused. Fulfilling this goal has not been easy. All too often terrorists who have fled the boundaries of the country where they committed their crimes have effectively escaped any threat of punishment. In some cases where they have been returned to the requesting country, and have been prosecuted and punished, the method of rendition employed has raised serious questions of rights violation.

This study attempts to explore both law and practice regarding the apprehension, prosecution, and punishment of terrorists. To this end the first part of the study considers the legal framework of the process. The legal framework includes international law, the law of the United States and the law of selected foreign countries. Accordingly, the first part of the study entails an examination or treaties—global, regional, and bilateral— declarations of the United Nations and other international bodies; customary rules of international law; United States statutes, court decisions, and regulations; and statutes, court decisions, and regulations of selected foreign countries.

The second part of the study first examines, to the extent data are available, state practice in an effort to add an empirical dimension. The state practice examined includes methods states actually employ to return terrorists to the place where they have allegedly committed their crimes. These methods, the generic term for which is "rendition," include formal extradition, exclusion and deportation—the so-called informal methods, and illegal abduction and seizure.

The study next explores the extent to which states have actually prosecuted and punished international terrorists—those who have been rendered back to the requesting country and those who have remained in the requested country after a decision on that country's part not to return the terrorist. Here the effort will be to determine both the United States' experience and the experience of selected foreign countries, with no pretense to being exhaustive, especially regarding the foreign experience. The hope is, however, that the sample will be extensive enough to aid in the identification of major trends.

A final section is devoted to conclusions and recommendations regarding law and practice. Extradition is considered, along with changes that might be made in United States law and practice and international initiatives that might be undertaken. Deportation and exclusion under United States law and foreign law and practice are examined, as well as the possibility that a common standard for all legal methods of rendition—formal and informal—might be developed and incorporated into appropriate international legal instruments. Lastly, possible reforms in international judicial assistance in criminal matters are evaluated, and the problem posed by safe-heaven states is briefly considered.

Terrorism: The Definitional Focus

"Terrorism" is a term of uncertain legal content. The late Richard Baxter, Professor of International Law at Harvard University and United States Judge on the International Court of Justice, was particularly dubious regarding the desirability and necessity of defining the term. In his view, "We have cause to regret that a legal concept of 'terrorism' was ever inflicted upon us. The term is imprecise; it is ambiguous; and above all, it serves no operative legal purpose."[3]

4   Introduction: Overview and Background

At the international level, in particular, there is no agreed-upon definition of "terrorism" and hence no international crime of terrorism. Rather, as we shall see more extensively in chapter 1, there are treaty provisions for suppression of aircraft hijacking; unlawful acts against the safety of civil aviation; unlawful acts against internationally protected persons, including diplomatic agents; the taking of hostages; and the theft of nuclear materials. Although these treaty provisions are often loosely described as "antiterrorist," the acts they cover are criminalized regardless of whether they, in any particular case, could be classified as "terrorism." Similarly, under national law, penal provisions with respect to murder, assault, theft, illegal detention of persons, taking of hostages, arson, and so on, are normally the basis for prosecution of "terrorist" acts, although they usually contain no reference to terrorism and are applicable notwithstanding the absence of a "terror" outcome. To be sure, some states have adopted antiterrorist statutes, but these are exceptions to the norm and are themselves highly controversial.

Besides being "imprecise," "ambiguous" and serving no "operative legal purpose," the term "terrorism" is emotionally charged, as demonstrated by the cliché, "One man's terrorism is another man's heroism." Some countries believe that the causes of terrorism or the political motivation of the individual terrorists are relevant to the problem of definition. For example, the position of some governments has been that individual acts of violence can be defined as terrorism only if they are employed solely for personal gain or caprice; acts committed in connection with a political cause, especially against colonialism and for national liberation, fall outside the definition and constitute legitimate measures of self-defense. Under this approach, then, the sending of letter bombs through the mails, hijacking of airplanes, kidnappings of or attacks on diplomats and international business persons, and the indiscriminate slaughter of civilians by members of revolutionary groups could never constitute "terrorism" if committed on behalf of a just cause.

Another approach is to define as terrorism only the use of terror by governments or so-called "state terrorism." Indeed, the word "terror" was first used in connection with the Jacobin "Reign of Terror" during the French Revolution. As a result of these pejorative and ideologically circumscribed uses of the term "terrorism" in international forums, no general definition has been agreed upon.

We shall return to the problem of defining terrorism elsewhere in this study. For present purposes, a rough working definition might be that currently employed by the United States government in collecting statistical information on international terrorist activity:

> *Terrorism* is premeditated, politically motivated violence perpetrated against noncombant targets by subnational groups or clandestine state agents.[4]

The United States government's definition of "international terrorism" is somewhat different from that adopted in this study:

International terrorism is terrorism involving citizens or territory of more than one country.[5]

As indicated above, the kind of "international terrorism" that is the focus of this study is terrorism committed by an individual in one country who then adds an international dimension to the problem by fleeing and seeking refuge in another country. We will not be directly concerned with the problem of state support of individual acts of terrorism, except insofar as such support frustrates efforts to apprehend, prosecute, and punish terrorists. Nor, as indicated above, will we be concerned with so-called "transnational terrorism" — that is, terrorism directed against foreign nationals, institutions, or governments within the boundary of a single state.

One more distinction between various types of terrorism may usefully be drawn: terrorism in armed conflict and international terrorism by private individuals. Terrorism in armed conflict includes acts inflicting terror in the context of "armed conflict" covered by the laws of war. Examples would include the killing of defenseless prisoners of war and the wanton slaughter of civilian noncombatants. International terrorism by private individuals covers acts outside of an "armed conflict." To be sure, these two categories are not necessarily mutually exclusive, as it may be difficult to determine whether a situation should be characterized as an "armed conflict" subject to the laws of war. Moreover, as we shall see later, several proposals have recently been made to bridge the gap between laws covering terrorism in armed conflict and terrorism committed by private individuals in the civilian context.

Notes

1. M. C. Bassiouni, "Ideologically Motivated Offenses and the Political Offenses Exception in Extradition — A Proposed Judicial Standard for an Unruly Problem," *De Paul Law Review* 19 (1969): 217, 228.
2. See J. Paust, *"Nonprotected" Persons or Things* in A. E. Evans and J. F. Murphy, eds, *Legal Aspects of International Terrorism* (Lexington, Mass.: Lexington Books, 1978), pp. 341, 360–61.
3. R. Baxter, *A Skeptical Look at the Concept of Terrorism, Akron Law Review* 7 (1974): 380.
4. *See*, e.g., Department of State, *Patterns of Global Terrorism* (September 1984).
5. Ibid.

PART ONE

Apprehension, Prosecution, and Punishment of Terrorists: The Legal Framework

CHAPTER 1

Counterterrorist Conventions — Aut Dedere, Aut Judicare

Several treaties or conventions have been concluded with specific reference to combating terrorism, although, as we shall see below, "terrorism" may not be explicitly mentioned by name. These treaties and conventions have been adopted at several levels. Some have been adopted by the United Nations or other international forums and are global in scope. Regional conventions concluded in Latin America and Western Europe and other areas are a product of the particular social, political, and cultural traditions of states in the region. Bilateral arrangements reflect the state of relations between the two countries concerned and are limited in their scope to particular manifestations of international terrorism. Although many of these conventions and treaties call for international cooperation in the prevention of terrorism as well, their primary thrust is towards the apprehension, prosecution, and punishment of terrorists.

Global Conventions

At this writing, the United Nations or U.N.-related agencies have adopted six counterterrorist conventions. These include the three conventions adopted under the auspices of the International Civil Aviation Organization—that is, the Convention on Offenses and Certain Acts Committed on Board Aircraft (Tokyo Convention);[1] The Convention for the Suppression of Unlawful Seizure of Aircraft (Hague Convention);[2] and The Convention for the Suppression of Unlawful Acts Against the Safety of Civilian Aviation (Montreal Convention).[3] The United Nations itself has adopted The Convention on the Prevention and Punishment of Crimes Against Internationally Protected Persons, Including Diplomatic Agents (New York

Convention);[4] and The International Convention Against the Taking of Hostages (Hostages Convention).[5] The Convention on the Physical Protection of Nuclear Material (Convention on Nuclear Material) was concluded under the auspices of the International Atomic Energy Agency.[6]

These conventions establish a framework for international cooperation among states to prevent and suppress international terrorism. To accomplish this goal, the New York Convention, for example, requires states parties to cooperate in order to prevent within their territories preparations for attacks on diplomats within or outside their territories, to exchange information, and to coordinate administrative measures against such attacks.[7] If an attack against an internationally protected person takes place, and an alleged offender has fled the country where the attack occurred, states parties are to cooperate in the exchange of information concerning the circumstances of the crime and the alleged offender's identity and whereabouts.[8] The state party where the alleged offender is found is obliged to take measures to ensure his presence for purposes of extradition or prosecution and to inform interested states and international organizations of the measure taken. Finally, states parties are to cooperate in assisting criminal proceedings brought for attacks on internationally protected persons, including supplying all relevant information at their disposal.[10]

The key feature of these conventions requires a state party that apprehends an alleged offender in its territory to either extradite him or submit his case to its authorities for purposes of prosecution.[11] Strictly speaking, none of these conventions alone creates an obligation to extradite. Rather, they contain an *inducement* to extradite by requiring the submission of alleged offenders for prosecution if extradition fails. Moreover, a legal *basis* for extradition is provided either by the convention, or through incorporation of the offenses mentioned in the convention into existing or future extradition treaties between the parties.[12] To varying degrees, the conventions also obligate the parties to take the important practical step of attempting to apprehend the accused offender and hold him in custody.[13]

The most important goal of these provisions is to ensure that the accused is prosecuted. To this end the alternative obligation to submit for prosecution is stated quite strongly in these conventions.[14] The obligation, however, is not to *try* the accused much less to punish him, but to submit the case to be considered for prosecution by the appropriate national prosecuting authority. If the criminal justice system lacks integrity, the risk of political intervention in the prosecution or at trial exists. Such intervention may prevent the trial, a conviction, or the appropriate punishment of the accused.

Even if the criminal justice system functions with integrity, it may be very difficult to obtain the evidence necessary to convict when the alleged offense was committed in a foreign country. This very practical impediment to conviction can be removed between states of goodwill only by patient and sustained efforts to develop and expand "judicial assistance" and other forms of cooperation between the law enforcement and judicial systems of different countries. The conventions create an obligation to cooperate in this respect but, as we shall see in greater detail later, this obligation poses major problems for even good faith efforts among countries with different types of legal systems.[15]

The United Nations Convention Against the Taking of Hostages adds a new dimension to presently existing international legal resources to combat terrorism by attempting to bridge the gap between the law of armed conflict and the law relating to private acts of individual terrorism. The convention seeks to ensure that international acts of hostage taking will be covered either by the convention itself or by one of the applicable conventions on the law of armed conflict.[16] For example, hostage taking is a "grave breach" of the 1949 Geneva Convention on the Prosecution of Civilians.[17] Other proposals to bridge the gap still further will be discussed later in this study.

Regional Conventions

At this writing, three conventions with a regional scope have been adopted in an effort to combat international terrorism. These include the Convention to Prevent and Punish the Acts of Terrorism Taking the Form of Crimes Against Persons and Related Extortion That Are of International Significance (OAS Convention);[18] The European Convention on the Suppression of Terrorism (The European Convention);[19] and The Agreement on the Application of the European Convention for the Suppression of Terrorism (the Dublin Agreement).[20] The three conventions are strikingly different in their scope and basic purpose.

CONVENTION TO PREVENT AND PUNISH THE ACTS OF TERRORISM TAKING THE FORM OF CRIMES AGAINST PERSONS AND RELATED EXTORTION THAT ARE OF INTERNATIONAL SIGNIFICANCE (OAS CONVENTION)

Despite its sweeping title, the OAS Convention is limited in its scope to internationally protected persons and has largely, although not entirely, been superseded by the United Nations Convention on Internationally Protected Persons.[21] Article 1 of the OAS Convention obligates states parties to cooperate "to prevent and punish acts of terrorism, especially kidnapping, murder, and other assaults against the life or physical integrity of those persons to whom the state has the duty according to international law to give special protection, as well as extortion in connection with those crimes." By this reference to other sources of international law, the convention leaves unsettled the issue whether it encompasses such persons as visiting ministers, legislators, governors of states or provinces, officials of a foreign government or an international public organization acting in their official capacities, and family members residing with or accompanying any of these persons. Negotiating history indicates that this convention was not intended to deal with crimes against a class this large,[22] and in any event, extending special protection to a class of this size would be a practical impossibility for most countries. Precisely how far the convention's scope of protection does extend is a matter of conjecture.

The convention is also ambiguous concerning the persons to be deterred from or punished for attacks on diplomats. By its terms, the convention appears to cover only principals involved in the crimes covered by the convention, and not persons who are co-conspirators and accessories not directly involved in the proscribed acts.[23] On the other hand, some commentators have suggested that an injured government might read the convention broadly to include all members of a political group in which the perpetrators and their assistants belong, thus violating fundamental human rights.[24]

The convention's key provisions are those that focus on extradition or punishment through national legislation of alleged offenders. First, the convention classifies the proscribed acts as "common crimes of international significance, regardless of motive."[25] On its face, the purpose of this classification seems to be to exclude violent attacks against diplomats from the political offense exception in extradition law and practice. According to the Inter-American Juridical Committee, "the political and ideological pretexts utilized as justification for these crimes in no way mitigate their cruelty and irrationality or the ignoble nature of the means employed and in no way remove their character as acts in violation of essential human rights."[26] Other provisions of the convention, however, cast doubt on the conclusion that the "political offense" exception to extradition is unavailable to states parties. Specifically, article 3 provides that "it is the exclusive responsibility of a state under whose jurisdiction or protection such persons are located to determine the nature of the acts and decide whether the standards of this convention are applicable." Although some have interpreted this provision as authorizing a state party only to determine whether the proscribed acts actually occurred, and not to classify the acts in terms of the political offense/common crime distinction,[27] article 3 must be read in light of article 6 of the convention. Article 6 provides, in categorical terms, that none of the convention's provisions "shall be interpreted so as to impair the right of asylum." The elimination of attacks on diplomats from the political offense category would perforce affect extradition practice and the right of asylum as they currently exist in much of Latin America. At a minimum, this apparent conflict of provisions creates a major ambiguity as to the continued viability of the political offense doctrine under the convention.

Under article 5, if extradition is denied "because the person sought is a national of the requested state, or because of some other legal or constitutional impediment, that state is obliged to submit the case to its competent authorities for prosecution as if the act had been committed in its territory." States parties are also obliged, under article 8(d), to "endeavor to have the criminal acts contemplated in this convention included in their penal laws, if not already so included." At first blush, these provisions might appear to assure severe punishments for persons who attack diplomats. In fact, however, if it decides not to extradite, a state party is entirely free to decline to prosecute an alleged offender without violating the convention. As noted above in the case of the United Nations conventions, the obligation on the state party is only to submit the accused to the appropriate authorities for the purpose of prosecution. Once the case is in the hands of government attorneys, they retain complete discretion as to whether to bring the case to trial. While their decisions may be based on such traditional grounds as insufficiency of evidence, or unavailability of witnesses, they may also turn on considerations of political expediency clothed in legal terms.[28]

EUROPEAN CONVENTION ON THE SUPPRESSION OF TERRORISM (EUROPEAN CONVENTION)

The European Convention attempts to deal directly with a primary problem in combating terrorism, the political offense exception to international extradition—a problem we will be exploring in various parts of this study. To this end, in article 1, the convention provides:

> For the purposes of extradition between Contracting States, none of the following offenses shall be regarded as a political offense or as an offense connected with a political motive or as an offense inspired by political motives:
>
> (a) an offense within the scope of the Convention for the Suppression of Unlawful Seizure of Aircraft, signed at the Hague on 16 December 1970;
> (b) an offense within the scope of the Convention for the Suppression of Unlawful Acts Against the Safety of Civil Aviation, signed at Montreal on 23 September 1971;
> (c) a serious offense involving an attack against the life, physical integrity or liberty of internationally protected persons, including diplomatic agents;
> (d) an offense involving kidnapping, taking of a hostage or serious unlawful detention;
> (e) an offense involving the use of a bomb, grenade, rocket, automatic firearm or letter or parcel bomb if this use endangers persons;
> (f) an attempt to commit any of the foregoing offenses or participation as an accomplice of a person who commits or attempts to commit such an offense.

Under article 2, the convention invites states parties to exclude additional acts of violence against persons or property from the political offense exception.[29] At the same time, article 13 of the convention allows states parties to register a reservation permitting them to reject a request for extradition on the ground that the offense is of a political character—notwithstanding that a listed offense is involved:

> provided that it undertakes to take into consideration when evaluating the character of the offense any particularly serious aspects of the offense including:
> (a) that it created a collective danger to the life, physical integrity or liberty of persons; or
> (b) that it affected persons foreign to the motives behind it; or
> (c) that cruel or viscious means had been used in the commission of the offense.

The convention also allows a requested state to refuse to extradite an accused under the following provision:

> Nothing in this convention shall be interpreted as imposing an obligation to extradite if the requested state has substantial grounds for believing that the request for extradition for an offense mentioned in Article 1 or 2 has been made for the purpose of prosecuting or punishing a person on account of his race, religion, nationality, or political opinion, or that the person's position may be prejudiced for any of these reasons.[30]

Should a state decide not to extradite an offender covered by the convention, the principle of *aut dedere, aut judicare* is applicable. Under article 7, a state party, if it fails to extradite, must "submit the case, without exception whatsoever and without undue delay, to its competent authorities for the purpose of prosecution. Those authorities shall take their decision in the same manner as in the case of any serious offense of a serious nature under the law of that State." To reinforce article 7, states parties are also obliged to amend their rules of criminal jurisdiction to allow them to try such an offender (provided that they recognize the principle of jurisdiction upon which the requesting state has based a request for extradition).[31]

Although the convention is an antiterrorism initiative, it nowhere attempts to define international terrorism. Rather, its approach, as we have seen above, is to list a series of crimes that states parties are to exclude, as between themselves, from the political offense exception to extradition. The convention is not itself an extradition agreement, but attempts to modify existing bilateral and multilateral extradition arrangements between its states parties. In attepting to exclude a variety of common crimes as well as "terrorism" from the political offense exception to extradition, the convention may have attempted too much. A number of states have, upon signing or ratifying the convention, reserved the right to refuse to extradite for an offense which they consider as political.[32] Ireland, which alone among member states of the Council of Europe has not even signed the convention, has gone so far as to claim that it is prohibited by its constitution from ratifying the convention. Under Article 29 of its constitution, "Ireland accepts the generally accepted principles of international law as its rule of conduct in its relations with other states." In Ireland's view, customary international law prevents the extradition of political offenders because it would be inconsistent with political asylum.[33] Ireland's position is controversial, and not widely accepted by other states. However, it demonstrates the risk of wide-ranging attempts to eliminate the political offense exception from extradition law and practice.

Moreover, France had failed to ratify the convention although it was an initial signatory. The election of President Mitterand in May 1981 makes future French ratification of the convention highly unlikely because the French Left has traditionally opposed the extradition of political offenders, and an early presidential act of Mitterand was to block the extradition to Spain of a Basque Fatherhood and Liberty (ETA) member, Tomas Linaza, in response to charges of murder. This was done although a French court had ruled earlier that France could extradite Mr. Linaza in keeping with French extradition law.[34] At this writing, there are 12 parties to the convention. However, in addition to France and Ireland, several other member states of the Council of Europe have failed to ratify.[35] Consequently, as we shall see more fully later in this study, the European Convention has been of limited significance.

AGREEMENT ON APPLICATION OF THE EUROPEAN CONVENTION FOR THE SUPPRESSION OF TERRORISM (DUBLIN AGREEMENT)

The Dublin agreement,[36] sponsored by the European Community, attempts to tighten application of the European Convention's extradite or prosecute formula to terrorist acts in two ways. First, under the agreement member states of the Community accept the proposition that in extradition proceedings between two member states, the European Convention will apply in full (that is, without reservations) *even if* one or both of the states is not a party to it, or if one or both has made a political offense reservation.[37] Second, the agreement seeks to restrict still further the effect of such reservations between member states of the Community. Hence, reservations made to the European Convention will not apply in extradition proceedings between EC member states, unless a further declaration to this effect is made.[38] Also, states parties to the Dublin Agreement that are not parties to the European Convention are required to indicate by declaration if they wish to retain the political offense defense in extradition proceedings between EC member states.[39] However, all nine member states of the European Community (as it then was) are required to ratify the convention before it comes into force.[40] France has declined to ratify and appears unlikely to do so.[41]

Bilateral Agreements

In addition to the global and regional multilateral conventions against terrorism discussed aboove, there are several bilateral agreements specifically directed against aircraft hijacking or the hijacking of ships.[42] Perhaps the most interesting example of such bilateral agreements is the United States-Cuba Memorandum of Understanding on Hijacking of Aircraft and Vessels and Other Offenses.[43] It provides that any person who hijacks an aircraft or vessel registered under the law of one party to the territory of the other party shall either be returned to the party of registry or "be brought before the courts of the party whose territory he reached for trial in conformity with its laws for the offense punishable by the most severe penalty according to the circumstances and seriousness of the acts to which the Article refers."[44] Thus, the memorandum incorporates the extradite or prosecute formula, but does so in a more meaningful way than do the multilateral antiterrorist conventions. Unlike the multilateral conventions, the United States-Cuba Memorandum requires that the accused actually be tried and not merely submitted "for the purpose of prosecution."

Under the United States-Cuba Memorandum each party expressly recognizes an affirmative obligation to prevent the use of its territory as a base for committing the illegal acts covered by the memorandum.[45] Each party must try "with a view to serve punishment" any person who,

> within its territory, hereafter conspires to promote, or promotes, or prepares, or directs, or forms part of an expedition which from its territory or any other place carries out acts of violence or deprivation against aircraft or vessels of any kind or registration coming from or going to the territory of the other party or . . . carries out such acts or other similar unlawful acts in the territory of the other party.[46]

Finally, the United States-Cuba Memorandum severely limits the extent to which the party where the hijacker arrives may take his motivation into account. It provides, in pertinent part, that there may be taken

> into consideration any extenuating or mitigating circumstances in those cases in which the persons responsible for the acts were being sought for strictly political reasons and were in real and imminent danger of death without a viable alternative for leaving the country, provided there was no financial extortion or physical injury to the members of the crew, passengers, or other persons in connection with the hijacking.[47]

In 1976, the memorandum was denounced by Cuba on the ground that the United States had failed to control anti-Castro terrorists who had planted a bomb on a Cuban civilian aircraft.[48] Nonetheless, in practice since this time, Cuba has shown that hijackers still face imprisonment in Cuba or extradition to the United States.[49]

Sanctions Against the Harboring of Hijackers

In terms of implementation, some of the counterterrorist conventions discussed above provide for third-party settlement of disputes regarding interpretation or application of the conventions, including possible reference to the International Court of Justice.[50] Nonetheless, it has been difficult to ensure compliance with these conventions. Some of the states parties have made reservations with respect to the articles on settlement of disputes.[51] There is, moreover, no way to ensure that states will become parties to the conventions, although moral pressure on them to do so may be somewhat effective. Other states which are parties to the relevant conventions may, when faced with actual terrorist incidents, decide for a variety of reasons not to honor their obligations, and none of the conventions contains provisions regarding coercive sanctions against states not parties to the conventions whose actions interfere with the conventions' successful operation.

The problem has been particularly acute with respect to aircraft hijacking where several states are prepared to give the hijacker a safe haven. Because of the perception that aircraft hijackings are an especially significant threat to the safety of civil aviation, there have been several attempts to develop new international legal instruments that would provide for sanctions in the form of suspension of air traffic with states which harbor hijackers or others who commit terrorist acts against civil aviation. The primary forum for these actions has been the International Civil Aviation Organization (ICAO).

Initiatives in ICAO have taken many forms. The United States proposed the adoption of a draft convention aimed at states which provided a safe-haven for persons who had committed acts of unlawful seizure of aircraft or other acts of unlawful interference with international civil aviation.[52] Under the convention, if a state party described as "an interested party" had reason to believe that a hijacker was within the territory of another state and that state had failed to extradite the hijacker or submit his case to the competent authorities for the purpose of prosecution, the interested party would be able to seek from a factfinding commission to be established by the convention a determination that the state harboring the alleged offender was violating its obligations. In cases where a determination of violation of the convention had been made, the United States draft convention provided for a meeting of interested air services states to decide upon what action should be taken with respect to the defaulting state. This action could have included the suspension of all international air navigation to and from the defaulting state. Such action might be taken against a state regardless of whether it was a party to the convention or a party to Hague Convention. A decision to take action would have been binding on all states parties to the convention and would have superseded any obligations those states might have had as to the defaulting state under any other international air transport agreement.

Another approach was a joint United Kingdom/Swiss proposal for an amendment to the Convention on International Civil Aviation (the "Chicago Convention"), the "umbrella" treaty covering rights and obligations of countries involved in international civil aviation. This proposal would have inserted a new chapter in the Chicago Convention which would set forth the basic obligations of the Tokyo, Hague, and Montreal conventions. Procedures for the settlement of disputes under the Chicago Convention would apply to this new chapter as well as to the rest of the Convention. These dispute settlement procedures require the Council of ICAO to adjudicate on any dispute concerning the interpretation or application of the convention with the right of appeal to the International Court of Justice. Under Article 87 of the Chicago Convention, each contracting state must bar the operation of an airline of a contracting state through the air space above its territory if the council has decided that the contracting state concerned is not fulfilling a final decision rendered by the Council under the settlement of dispute provisions of the convention. The assembly of ICAO is required under Article 88 to suspend the voting power in the assembly and in the council of any contracting state found to have violated its obligations under the convention. The United Kingdom/Swiss proposal would have amended article 87 so as to require contracting states not to allow the operation of an airline of a contracting state through the airspace of their territories when the council had decided *either* that the contracting state was not conforming to a final decision rendered by the council *or* that the contracting state had breached its obligations under the new chapter to be inserted in the convention and containing the provisions of the Tokyo, Hague, and Montreal conventions.

Under the United Kingdom/Swiss amendments, if a contracting state had reason to believe that another contracting state had not complied with its obligations either to extradite or prosecute an alleged offender under the Tokyo, Hague or Montreal conventions, or to return the aircraft and allow the crew and passengers to continue their journey, it could have submitted the issue to the council of ICAO. The council would then have decided whether these allegations were correct. Upon a decision of the council that they were, all contracting states would have been obliged to prevent any airline of the contracting state concerned flying into the airspace over their territories. Additionally, the assembly of ICAO would also have had the right to suspend the voting power of the defaulting contracting state in the assembly and the council.

The Soviet Union proposed that the Hague and Montreal conventions be amended so that states parties would no longer have the choice either to extradite or submit to prosecution an offender found in their territory. Instead, states would have been obliged to accede to any request for extradition except when the offender was a national of the requested state.

These and other proposals for sanctions arrangements were discussed at an ICAO Diplomatic Conference and Extraordinary Assembly held at Rome from August 28 to September 21, 1973. Despite strenuous efforts by those supporting international sanctions against states harboring aircraft hijackers, no proposal succeeded in obtaining the necessary two-thirds majority for adoption. With this failure, it was clear that efforts in ICAO to establish arrangements for sanctions would be unavailing.

THE BONN DECLARATION

Efforts in ICAO having failed, an initiative outside of the United Nations was undertaken. On July 17, 1978, the heads of state and government participating in the Bonn Economic Summit (Canada, France, the Federal Republic of Germany, Italy, Japan, the United Kingdom, and the United States) agreed upon a declaration generally called the Bonn Declaration on Hijacking.[53] The declaration provides:

> The Heads of State and Government, concerned about terrorism and the taking of hostages, declare that their governments will intensify their joint efforts to combat international terrorism. To this end, in cases where a country refuses extradition or prosecution of those who have hijacked an aircraft and/or does not return such aircraft, the Heads of State and Government are jointly resolved that their governments shall take immediate action to cease all flights to that country. At the same time, their governments will initiate action to halt all in-coming flights from that country, or from any country of the airlines of the country concerned. They urge other governments to join them in the commitment.

Although there is some disagreement on this point, most commentators agree that the Bonn Declaration is not a binding legal instrument, but rather a statement of policy which expresses the intent of the heads of state and government concerned to take action when there has been a hijacking and states have failed to live up to their obligations.[54] The scope of the declaration is wide, since if a state is in violation of its obligations, the heads of state and government have expressed their intention to cease all flights to and from that country and to halt all in-coming flights from any country by the airlines of that country. Follow-up efforts have succeeded in obtaining widespread support for the declaration and in inducing additional countries to become parties to the ICAO Conventions.

The first test of the Bonn Declaration came on July 20, 1981. At that time, the heads of state and government meeting at the Ottawa Economic Summit considered the hijacking in March of 1981 of Pakistan International Airlines aircraft to Afghanistan. Recalling and reaffirming the principles set forth in the 1978 Bonn Declaration, the heads of state and government stated that the action of the Afghan regime, both during the incident and subsequently in giving refuge to the hijackers "was and is a flagrant breach of its international obligations under the Hague Convention to which Afghanistan is a party and constitutes a serious threat to air safety."[55] Accordingly, heads of state and government proposed to "suspend all flights to and from Afghanistan in implementation of the Bonn Declaration unless Afghanistan immediately takes steps to comply with its obligations."[56] They also called upon "all states which share their concern for air safety to take appropriate action to persuade Afghanistan to honor its obligations."[57]

The United States favored an immediate application of the Bonn Declaration sactions. However, France, the Federal Republic of Germany, and the United Kingdom, which were the only countries among the seven to whose territories Ariana Afghan Airlines flew, were of the opinion that they could not employ such sanctions without violating the terms of their bilateral air transit agreements with Afghanistan. Accordingly, these governments instead gave Afghanistan a year's notice of their intent to terminate these agreements.[58]

On November 30, 1982, these three countries implemented the Bonn Declaration by terminating all air traffic with Afghanistan.[59] Scholars have questioned whether the Bonn Declaration can be implemented consistently with the obligations of the Summit Countries to other states under the International Air Services Transit Agreement, the Chicago Convention, and bilateral aviation agreements.[60] In this instance, the bilateral aviation agreements between Afghanistan and the United Kingdom, the Federal Republic of Germany, and France pose no problem because they have been terminated in accordance with their terms. Similarly, no difficulty is likely to arise under the International Air Services Transit Agreement or the Chicago Convention, since these agreements cover overflights and emergency landings, neither of which is expected to be involved in the case of Afghanistan. Nor is the application of the sanctions provided for in the Bonn Declaration likely to affect third states — which are non-signatories of the declaration and which are not the targets of sanctions.

This happy congruence of circumstances, however, will not necessarily be present in future cases, and these legal question marks regarding the declaration remain. Moreover, application of the sanctions against

Afghanistan is likely to have little economic impact. More generally, past experience with economic sanctions against Rhodesia and South Africa does not give cause for optimism that application of the Bonn Declaration sanctions will be effective in inducing the target country to cease its support for terrorist activity. Consequently, the primary value of the Bonn Declaration, and of its application to Afghanistan, is likely to be the symbolic effect of a united stand against terrorism on the part of the summit countries.

Still, the legal barriers to implementation of the Bonn Declaration are not insurmountable, and a legal counsellor of the United Kingdom's Foreign and Commonwealth Office has recently argued convincingly that they could be overcome if the political will to apply the Bonn Declaration sanctions is present.[61] Whether the political determination of governments to take action in any particular case will be present remains to be seen.

Implementation: National Legislation and Court Decisions

As noted above, many of the counterterrorist conventions require that states parties adopt implementing legislation in order to establish their jurisdiction over covered manifestations of international terrorism if they decide not to extradite the alleged offender. This is a crucial innovation, because the normal extradition treaty contains no such requirement, and, as a result, if the alleged offender is not extradited, he escapes prosecution entirely.

In this subsection we explore first United States statutes, as well as court decisions arising thereunder, and then the pattern in selected foreign countries.

THE UNITED STATES

Crimes Against Aviation

The Tokyo (article 3), Hague (articles 2, 4), and Montreal (articles 3, 5, 10) conventions have placed an obligation on states parties to enact legislation sufficient to carry out their responsibilities thereunder. The United States, a party to all three conventions, has now enacted legislation to carry out its obligations under all of them.

Specifically, the Anti-Hijacking Act of 1974 amended the Federal Aviation Act of 1948 to redefine the "special aircraft jurisdiction of the United States" and to revise the offense of "aircraft piracy" to conform to the requirements of the Hague Convention.[62] It also conferred jurisdiction upon United States federal courts to try alleged offenders under the statute, regardless of where their alleged hijackings took place, and provided for the death penalty or life imprisonment when the death of another person results from the commission or attempted commission of the offense. Similarly, the act requires a minimum sentence of twenty years or a fine of $10,000 for interference with flight crew; up to life if a dangerous weapon is used in the act; and a prison term of up to one year and a fine of $10,000 for conveying false information about hijacking or an attempted hijacking—up to five years and a fine of $5,000 if done maliciously or in reckless disregard of the safety of human life.

The act grants the Federal Aviation Administration exclusive responsibility for any law enforcement activity affecting the safety of persons aboard aircraft involved in the commission or attempted commission of aircraft hijacking and prohibits, except as otherwise provided by law, the transfer or assignment of those responsibilities. Other federal departments and agencies are required, upon FAA request, to "provide such assistance as may be necessary to carry out the purposes (of the law enforcement activity)."

In addition to the provisions relating to criminal matters, the act authorizes the imposition of sanctions against states which fail to take measures necessary to combat aircraft hijacking. For example, the act authorizes the president to suspend air service between the United States and any state that:

> is acting in a manner inconsistent with the Convention for the Suppression of Unlawful Seizure of Aircraft, or if he determines that a foreign nation permits the use of territory under its jurisdiction as a base of operations or training or as sanctuary for, or in any way arms, aids, or abets, any terrorist organization which knowingly uses the illegal seizure of aircraft or threat thereof as an instrument of policy . . .

Also, the act provides for the maintenance of minimum security measures in foreign air transportation and grants the secretary of transportation, subject to the approval of the secretary of state, authority to "withhold, revoke, or impose conditions on the operating authority of the airlines of (any nation he finds 'does not effectively maintain and administer security measures . . . equal to or above the minimum standards established pursuant to the Convention on International Aviation')."

Provisions of the United States Criminal Code establish felony offenses involving the destruction of aircraft and aircraft facilities. Section 2011 to 2015 of the Comprehensive Crime Control Act of 1984, the "Aircraft Sabotage Act," constitutes implementing legislation enabling the United States to discharge its obligations fully under the Montreal Convention.

United States courts have enforced the Anti-Hijacking Act of 1974 with consistency. As of January 1, 1983, of the 353 persons involved in 256 hijackings of United States registered aircraft, 238 have been apprehended.[63] Of this number, 141 have been convicted in the United States, 5 acquitted, 20 have had charges dismissed or prosecution declined, and 11 cases are pending.[64] Moreover, as we shall see in chapter 6, penalties imposed for aircraft hijacking, kidnapping and interference with the flight crew have been severe.

Crimes Against Internationally Protected Persons

United States expansion of the scope of its federal legislation on the protection of diplomats and diplomatic premises preceded adoption of the United Nations convention on internationally protected persons.[65] In 1972, the United States adopted amendments to its federal criminal code whose primary purpose was to afford United States jurisdiction, concurrent with that of the states, to proceed against those who violate diplomatic inviolability. Under the law as it existed prior to the amendments, in most cases of attacks on diplomats, the federal government could do little more than encourage local enforcement of the law.

The 1972 amendment extend federal criminal jurisdiction to cover a variey of attacks on diplomatic personnel and diplomatic premises. For example, under section 1116 of Title 18 of the United States code, criminal penalties of up to life imprisonment are provided for anyone who kills a "foreign official," a term that covers high-ranking officials of foreign governments and international organizations, as well as members of their families who accompany them, or an "official guest." Section 1116 defines an official guest as a "citizen or national from a foreign country present in the United States as an official guest of the government of the United States pursuant to designation as such by the Secretary of State." Thus, foreign citizens who might come to the United States as members of an Olympic contingent could be designated "official guests" by the secretary of state and thereby become entitled to special protection under federal law. Not surprisingly, a primary motivating factor behind the introduction of this provision was the 1972 murder of the Israeli Olympic competitors at Munich. Its relevance to the 1984 Olympics in Los Angeles is self-evident.

Another especially noteworthy provision of the 1972 Amendments is revised section 1201 of Title 18, which expands federal jurisdiction over kidnapping. Under revised section 1201, federal jurisdiction is provided when: (1) the victim is transported in interstate or foreign commerce (as under the law as it existed prior to 1972); (2) the kidnapping occurs within the special maritime and territorial jurisdiction of the United States; (3) in the special aircraft jurisdiction of the United States; or (4) the victim is a "foreign official" or an "official guest" as defined in section 1116 of Title 18.

The drafters of the 1972 amendments clearly intended that these provisions should supplement and not preempt state law and practice on murder, kidnapping, and assault. Primary responsibility to investigate, prosecute, and punish these common-law crimes remains with the states.

The Convention on the Prevention and Punishment of Crimes Against Internationally Protected Persons, Including Diplomatic Agents (New York Convention) was adopted by the United Nations on December 14, 1973. Public Law 94-467 of October 8, 1976, implementing the New York and OAS conventions, further amended those sections of Title 18 which were changed by the 1972 amendments by adding "internationally protected persons" as a third category of individuals entitled to this special protection of the law. The 1976 amendments also added section 878 of Title 18, a new section which provides felony punishment for (1) willfully threatening to kill, kidnap or assault a foreign official, official guest or internationally protected person, and (2) making any extortionate demand in connection with any violation of sections 112, 1116, or 1201. The 1976 amendments also confer jurisdiction upon United States federal courts to try alleged offenders present within the United States regardless of the locality of their alleged crimes. Moreover, the 1976 amendments authorized the attorney general, in his enforcement of sections 1116, 1201, 112(a), or any conspiracy or attempt to commit offenses covered by those sections, to request assistance from "any federal, state, or local agency, including the army, navy, and airforce," thus providing an exception to the prohibition against use of military forces as *posse comitatus*.

Several interesting cases have arisen under the revised legislation. The 1972 revisions of the Federal Kidnapping Law got their first test in 1974 and 1975 in *United States v. Lechoco.*[66] In that case, Lechoco, an immigrant Philippine lawyer, armed with a pistol concealed in a briefcase, went to the Philippine Chancery on November 18, 1974, to keep an appointment he had previously made with the Philippine ambassador. After entering the ambassador's office, Lechoco took the ambassador hostage at gunpoint; threatened the ambassador's secretary at gunpoint; shot and wounded a Philippine Economic attaché; and fired at a District of Columbia metropolitan police officer. Lechoco initially demanded publicity for his acts and later also demanded the safe conduct of his son from the Philippines to Washington.

Lechoco held the Philippine ambassador hostage for over ten hours. He finally surrendered to metropolitan police and FBI agents after an agreement was reached with Philippine president Ferdinand Marcos to place Lechoco's son on the first available flight from Manila.

On June 19, 1975, Lechoco was convicted by a jury in the District Court for the District of Columbia of kidnapping of and assault on a foreign official. In the sentencing proceedings before the district judge, Lechoco's attorney, pleading for a light sentence, contended that this case should not be considered one of "political terrorism" because Lechoco's motivation in kidnapping the ambassador was to unite his family, and that the separation of Lechoco and his family had already imposed sufficient punishment on him.

In response, the government argued that Lechoco's actions were no different from those of numerous others who had hijacked planes or kidnapped diplomatic personnel. According to the government, Lechoco's intent to commit a terrorist act was shown by his bringing a gun and other terrorist equipment with him to the appointment with the ambassador. The government further pointed out that this was the first prosecution under the 1972 revisions of the federal kidnapping law and that the diplomatic community was vitally concerned that a severe penalty be imposed in order to deter future kidnappings of and other attacks on diplomatic personnel.

The court imposed a ten-year sentence on Lechoco under the federal kidnapping count, as well as shorter sentences under other counts, all to run concurrently. In so ruling, the court stated that the violent circumstances of the case "cannot be overshadowed by the natural sympathy which we have to extend to this defendant."[67] It further noted that "Congress considered this crime to be so abhorrent that it provided probation and split-sentence alternatives were not available to the court, thus mandating that the court impose a jail sentence. Under the terms of the statute itself, it must be for a term of years."[68]

The court also rejected Lechoco's motion that he be released on bond pending appeal. Taking note of the Bail Reform Act's standard of danger to the community or to another person or persons, the court was of the opinion that if Lechoco were released, the Philippine ambassador or his representative might be in danger, and that they should not be subjected to a "lingering fear" of attack from Lechoco. In support of this conclusion, the court stated that it was not convinced that Lechoco's sole motive in attacking the ambassador had been a concern for his son. According to the court, the record indicated that Lechoco was also motivated by a "long-standing hostility towards the Marcos' regime in the Philippines."[69]

In sum, then, the district court followed a hard-line approach in the Lechoco case, imposing a severe sentence and rejecting Lechoco's plea that he be released on bond pending an appeal. It is noteworthy that the question of Lechoco's motivation was not raised until the sentencing stage. The only defense raised during the trial was insanity. Hence the defense did not contend that Lechoco's motivation in kidnapping the ambassador could excuse his actions, but only that it might serve as a mitigating factor in the sentencing process.

With respect to sentencing, the court implied that Lechoco's motivation might be taken into account as a possible mitigating circumstance but found that he had failed to prove that his sole or even his primary motive in the kidnapping was to have his son reunited with him. The court also interpreted the federal statute in such a way as to limit its discretion in imposing a lenient sentence. Finally, the court stressed the interest of the Philippine Ambassador and Embassy, as well as that of the diplomatic community, in freedom from the threat or use of violence, as support for its conclusion that Lechoco should remain in jail pending appeal.

In *United States v. Layton*, the defendant, a United States citizen, was indicted on four criminal counts arising from events which resulted in the death of Congressman Leo J. Ryan in Guyana in 1978.[70] The defendant was charged under four counts: (1) conspiracy to murder a congressman under 18 U.S.C. §351(d); (2) aiding and abetting the murder of a congressman, under 18 U.S.C. §351(a)2; (3) conspiracy to murder an internationally protected person under 18 U.S.C. §1117; (4) aiding and abetting the attempted murder of an internationally protected person, under 18 U.S.C. §1116(a)2. The court held that it had subject matter jurisdiction over all these counts although the events on which they were based all occurred outside the territorial limits of the United States.

Citing, inter alia, *Blackmer v. United States*, the court in *Layton* upheld the constitutionality of Congress' applying United States criminal law extraterritorially.[71] In so ruling, the court discussed international law principles of criminal jurisdiction and indicated that application of United States law extraterritorially in this case could be based on the protective, the territorial (objective), passive personality, and nationality principles. The court then turned to the defendant's argument that the various statutory revisions should be interpreted in such a way as to rule out their application to the facts of this particular case. Among other things, defendant argued that 18 U.S.C. §1116(c) required the alleged offender to be present within the United States at the time of the indictment. Section 1116(c) provides in pertinent part:

> (c) If the victim of an offense under subsection (a) is an internationally protected person, the United States may exercise jurisdiction over the offense if the alleged offender is present within the United States irrespective of the place where the offense was committed or the nationality of the victim or the alleged offender. As used in this subsection, the United States includes all areas under the jurisdiction of the United States, including any of the places within the divisions of §§5 and 7 of this title . . .

The court agreed with the defendant that, in a case where the *only* basis for extraterritorial jurisdiction was the universality principle, the defendant would have to be present in the United States at the time of the indictment. But, the court concluded, this was not the case here because the legislative history of section 1116 indicated that Congress intended to fulfill United States obligations under the New York and OAS Conventions completely. The court noted that the New York Convention provides:

> Article 3. (1) Each State Party shall take such measures as may be necessary to establish jurisdiction over the crimes set forth in Article 2 in the following cases:

(a) when the crime is committed in the territory of that State or on board a ship or aircraft registered in that State;

(b) when the alleged offender is a national of that State;

(c) when the crime is committed against an internationally protected person as defined in Article 1 who enjoys his status as such by virtue of functions which he exercises on behalf of that State.

(2) Each State Party shall likewise take such measures as may be necessary to establish its jurisdiction over these crimes in cases where the alleged offender is present in its territory and it does not extradite him pursuant to Article 8 to any of the States mentioned in paragraph 1 of the Article.

(3) This Convention does not exclude any criminal jurisdiction exercised in accordance with internal law.

The court pointed out that Article 3 of the New York Convention sets forth four bases for the exercise of jurisdiction and that Congress, in enacting section 1116(c), had explicitly provided for the exercise of jurisdiction only under the fourth category. The court went on to hold, however, that Congress had implicitly provided for the exercise of jurisdiction under the three other bases and that it was only necessary to provide explicitly for jurisdiction based on universality since it depends, by its very nature, on the presence of the alleged offender within the state's territorial jurisdiction at the time of prosecution.

Finally, with respect to the conspiracy count, the court held that 18 U.S.C. §1117's reference to sections 1111, 1114, and 1116 included any explicit or implicit assertions of extraterritorial jurisdiction contained in these provisions as well.

The court in *In re Letelier v. Republic of Chile* allowed the plaintiffs to recover damages in tort against the government of Chile and individual defendants for the 1976 murder of Letelier, former Ambassador of Chile to the United States, by bomb explosion in Washington, D.C.[72] The court upheld this recovery on the ground that, *inter alia*, the plaintiff had a right of recovery based on "tortious actions in violation of international law" and the "tortious assault of an internationally protected person in violation of 18 U.S.C. §1116."[73] Section 1116 does not, by its terms, provide a tortious action for an attack on an internationally protected person, but the court nonetheless used the provision indirectly as part of the basis for the plaintiff's recovery in tort.

Hostage Taking and Theft of Nuclear Materials

On October 15, 1982, Congress adopted Public Law 97-351, §2(b), 96 Stat. 1666, 18 U.S.C. §831, which allows the United States to carry out its obligation under the Convention on the Physical Protection of Nuclear Material to prosecute those accused of certain serious offenses involving nuclear material if they fail to extradite them. Section 831(a) of title 18 provides that:

(a) Whoever, if one of the circumstances described in subsection (c) of this section occurs—

(1) without lawful authority, intentionally receives, possesses, uses, transfers, alters, disposes of, or disperses any nuclear material and—

(A) thereby knowingly causes the death of or serious bodily injury to any person or substantial damage to property; or

(B) knows that circumstances exist which are likely to cause the death of or serious bodily injury to any person or substantial damage to property;

(2) with intent to deprive another of nuclear material, knowingly—

(A) takes and carries away nuclear material of another without authority;

(B) makes an unauthorized use, disposition, or transfer, of nuclear material belonging to another; or

(C) uses fraud and thereby obtains nuclear material belonging to another;

(3) knowingly—

(A) uses force; or

(B) threatens or places another in fear that any person other than the actor will imminently be subject to bodily injury;

and thereby takes nuclear material belonging to another from the person or presence of any other;

(4) intentionally intimidates any person and thereby obtains nuclear material belonging to another;

(5) with intent to compel any person, international organization, or governmental entity to do or refrain from doing any act, knowingly threatens to engage in conduct described in paragraph (2)(A) or (3) of this subsection;

(6) knowingly threatens to use nuclear material to cause death or serious bodily injury to any person or substantial damage to property under circumstances in which the threat may reasonably be understood as an expression of serious purposes;

(7) attempts to commit an offense under paragraphs (1), (2), (3), or (4) of this subsection; or

(8) is a party to a conspiracy of two or more persons to commit an offense under paragraph (1), (2), (3), or (4) of this subsection, if any of the parties intentionally engaged in any conduct in furtherance of such offense;

shall be punished as provided in subsection (b) of this section.

The circumstances specified in subsection (c) include:

(1) the offense is committed in the United States or the special maritime and territorial jurisdiction of the United States, or the special aircraft jurisdiction of the United States (as defined in section 101 of the Federal Aviation Act of 1958 (49 U.S.C. 1301));

(2) the defendant is a national of the United States, as defined in section 101 of the Immigration and Nationality Act 8 U.S.C. 1101);

(3) at the time of the offense the nuclear material is in use, storage, or transport, for peaceful purposes, and after the conduct required for the offense occurs the defendant is found in the United States, even if the conduct required for the offense occurs outside the United States; or

(4) the conduct required for the offense occurs with respect to the carriage of a consignment of nuclear material for peaceful purposes by any means of transportation intended to go beyond the territory of the state where the shipment originates beginning with the departure from a facility of the shipper in that state and ending with the arrival at a facility of the receiver within the state of ultimate destination and either of such states is the United States.

Under subsection (b) of section 831 penalties of up to life imprisonment and a fine of not more than $250,000 may be imposed, depending on the precise nature of the offense and its gravity. Under carefully delineated circumstances, the attorney general may request and receive assistance from the secretary of defense if such assistance will not, in the opinion of the secretary of defense, adversely affect the military preparedness of the United States. Thus, as in the case of crimes against internationally protected persons, there is an exception to the prohibition against use of military forces as *posse comitatus*.

Sections 2001 and 2002 of the Comprehensive Crime Control Act of 1984 amend chapter 55 of Title 18 of the United States code by adding a new section 1203 on hostage taking. Under this amendment the federal kidnapping statute now provides for federal jurisdiction over any kidnapping with an international dimension in which a threat is made to kill, injure, or continue to detain a victim in order to compel a third party to do or abstain from doing something.

SELECTED FOREIGN COUNTRIES

As noted above, the United States has taken a piecemeal approach to the adoption of legislation to fulfill its obligations under the counterterrorism conventions it has ratified. That is, the United States has adopted legislation in specific reference to the acts criminalized under the conventions and usually has held up ratification of the conventions until adoption of implementing legislation.

The pattern in other countries varies greatly, and it is risky to generalize. Some countries have adopted legislation referring specifically to the counterterrorist conventions for purposes of defining the crime and establishing extraterritorial jurisdiction over it. For example, section 8 of the Danish penal code provides:

Section 8

1. Under Danish criminal jurisdiction shall also come acts committed outside the territory of the Danish State, irrespective of the nationality of perpetrator;

. . .

(5) where the act falls within the provisions of the Convention for the Suppression of Unlawful Acts Against the Safety of Civil Aviation; or

(6) where the act falls within the provisions of the Convention on the Prevention and Punishment of Crimes against Internationally Protected Persons, including Diplomatic Agents; or

(7) where the act falls within the provisions of the European Convention on Extradition and where a request for proceedings in this country has been submitted in pursuance of that Convention; or

(8) where the act falls within the provisions of Article 1 of the European Convention on the Suppression of Terrorism.

Section 183a

2. Any person who on board an aircraft unlawfully by force seizes control of the aircraft, interferes with the maneuvering thereof, shall be liable to imprisonment for a maximum period of twelve years.[74]

Other countries have adopted the United States approach. Writing in 1977, the late Alona Evans reported that, of 91 states surveyed, 34 had specific antihijacking legislation; 70 of these 91 states were bound by one or more of the three civil aviation counterterrorist conventions.[75] Similarly, this writer, reporting as of the same time, indicated that many, perhaps most, countries provided expressly in their penal codes that attempted attacks against diplomats are subject to severe criminal penalties, although the jurisdictional scope of many of these provisions was limited to attacks on diplomats taking place within the territory of the prosecuting state.[76]

Still other countries—e.g., Austria, Colombia, and Switzerland—have prosecuted acts that may be characterized as "terrorist," including hijacking and related attacks on civil aviation and attacks against internationally protected persons, under relevant general provisions of the state's criminal law or penal code. Moreover, the scope of some countries' legislation may be wide indeed. Under the penal code of Mexico, for example, crimes committed in foreign territory by a Mexican against a Mexican or against foreigners, or by a foreigner against a Mexican, are punished in the republic in accordance with federal laws, if the following requisites concur:

1. The accused is found in the Republic.

2. The accused has not been definitely judged in the country where he allegedly committed the crime.

3. The act committed is a crime under both the law of the place where committed and the law of Mexico.[77]

An even more expansive — perhaps the most expansive — exercise of extraterritorial criminal jurisdiction is to be found in the terms and recent application of a 1972 amendment to the Israeli penal law (Offenses Committed Abroad). The amendment provides in pertinent part:

The courts in Israel are competent to try under Israeli law a person who has committed abroad an act which would be an offense if it had been commited in Israel and which harmed or was intended to harm the State of Israel, its security, property or economy or its transport or communications link with other countries.[78]

Under this legislation, an Israeli military court in 1973 convicted Faik Bulut, a twenty-three-year-old turkish citizen, of the offense of belonging to Al-Fatah in Lebanon and Syria and sentenced him to seven years in prison. Bulut had been captured in February 1972 during an Israeli raid 100 miles into Lebanon. In response to contentions by defense counsel that the statute and its application violated international law, the court cited the protective principle in upholding the validity of the statute and ruled that Bulut's involuntary abduction from Lebanon without extradition did not preclude jurisdiction. Although the court expressly avoided relying on the universality principle, the prosecution and defense counsel argued as if it were a primary basis of jurisdiction.

The Israeli statute and its utilization in the Bulut case has been sharply criticized as an exercise of "exorbitant" jurisdiction under international law.[79] Be that as it may, it is beyond the scope of this study to discuss the validity of the Israeli statute under international law. It suffices for present purposes to note that, with Israeli ratification of the New York Convention, application of the statute to prosecute a person accused of attacking a diplomat abroad would be authorized and indeed demanded (in the case of refusal to extradite) by the terms of the convention.

The International Convention Against the Taking of Hostages and the Convention on the Physical Protection of Nuclear Material have been concluded too recently to allow any pattern to emerge as to their implementation. However, since hostage taking remains a prevalent manifestation of international terrorism, implementation of the Hostages Convention by arrest and extradition or prosecution may be expected at an early date. As cases arise involving possible application of the Hostages Convention, it will be interesting to note whether the convention, in practice, succeeds in closing any gap that may exist between legal coverage of hostage taking during armed conflict and that occurring in a situation involving violence not rising to the magnitude of armed conflict as that term is defined under the laws of war.

One hopes that the terms of the Convention on the Physical Protection of Nuclear Material are never invoked in the context of a terrorist event.

Notes

1. Convention on Offenses and Certain Other Acts Committed on Board Aircraft, done at Tokyo, Sept. 14, 1963, [1969] 20 U.S.T. 2941, T.I.A.S. No. 6768, 704 U.N.T.S. 219.
2. Convention for the Suppression of Unlawful Seizure of Aircraft, done at The Hague, Dec. 16, 1970, [19701] 22 U.S.T. 1641, T.I.A.S. No. 7192, 10 I.L.M. 133 (1971).
3. Convention for the Suppression of Unlawful Acts Against the Safety of Civil Aviation, done at Montreal, Sept. 23, 1971, [1973] 24 U.S.T. 565, T.I.A.S. No. 7570, 10 I.L.M. 1151 (1971).
4. Convention on the Prevention and Punishment of Crimes Against Internationally Protected Persons, Including Diplomatic Agents, done at New York (hereinafter Convention on Protected Persons), Dec. 14, 1973, 28 U.S.T. 1975, T.I.A.S. No. 8532.
5. International Convention Against the Taking of Hostages, 34 U.N. GAOR Supp. (No. 39) at 23, U.N. Doc. A/34/39 (1979), reprinted in 18 I.L.M. 1456 (1979).
6. Convention on the Physical Protection of Nuclear Material, opened for signature, Mar. 3, 1980, reprinted in 18 I.L.M. 1419, 1422-31 (1979).
7. Convention on Protected Persons, supra note 4, art. 4.
8. Id., art. 5, para. 2.
9. Id., art. 6.
10. Id., art. 10.
11. See, e.g., id., art. 7.
12. See, e.g., International Convention Against Hostage Taking, supra, note 5, art. 10.
13. See id., art. 8; Convention on Protected Persons, supra note 4, art. 6.
14. The strongest such provision is contained in the International Convention Against the Taking of Hostages, which provides:

> The State Party in the territory of which the alleged offender is found shall, if it does not extradite him, be obliged, without exception whatsoever and whether or not the offense was commited in its territory, to submit the case to its competent authorities for the purpose of prosecution, through proceedings in accordance with the laws of that State. *Those authorities shall take their decision in the same manner as in the case of any ordinary offense of a gross nature under the law of that state.*

International Convention Against Hostage Taking, supra note 5, art. 8 (emphasis added).
15. For an exploration of some of these problems, see Grutzner, "International Judicial Assistance and Cooperation in Criminal Matters," in M. C. Bassiouni and V. Nanda, eds., *A Treatise on International Criminal Law*, Vol. 2 (1973), p. 189.
16. Article 12 of the convention provides:

> In so far as the Geneva Convention of 1949 for the protection ow war victims or the Additional Protocols to those Conventions are applicable to a particular act of hostage-

taking, and in so far as States Parties to this Convention are bound under those Conventions to prosecute or hand over the hostage-taker, the present Convention shall not apply to an act of hostage taking committed in the course of armed conflicts as defined in the Geneva Conventions of 1949 and the Protocols thereto, including armed conflicts, mentioned in article 1, paragraph 4 of Additional Protocol I of 1977, in which peoples are fighting against colonial domination and alien occupation and against racist regimes in the exercise of their right of self-determination, as enshrined in the Charter of the United Nations and Declaration on Principles of International Law Concerning Friendly Relations and Co-operation among States in accordance with the Charter of the United Nations.

Convention Against the Taking of Hostages, supra note 5, art. 12.

17. Geneva Convention Relative to the Protection of Civilian Persons in Time of War, done at Geneva, Aug. 12, 1948, art. 147 [1956] 6 U.S.T. 3516, T.I.A.S. No. 3365, 75 U.N.T.S. 287.

18. Convention to Prevent and Punish the Acts of Terrorism Taking the Forms of Crimes Against Persons and Related Extortion that are of International Significance, done at Washington, D.C., Feb. 2, 1971, 27 U.S.T. 3949, T.I.A.S. No. 8413, OASTS 37, at 6, OAS Off. Doc. OEA/Ser. A/17 (hereinafter cited as OAS Convention).

19. European Convention on the Suppression of Terrorism, entered into force Oct. 25, 1978, Gr. Brit. T.S. No. 93 (Cmd. 7390), Europ. T.S. No. 90, reprinted in 15 I.L.M. 1272 (1976).

20. The text of the Dublin Agreement may be found at 19 I.L.M. 325 (1980).

21. This description of the OAS Convention is taken largely from Murphy, "Protected Persons and Diplomatic Facilities,' in A. E. Evans and J. F. Murphy, eds., *Legal Aspects of International Terrorism* (1978), pp. 277, 299–303.

22. See Comment, "The Inter-American Convention on the Kidnapping of Diplomats," *Columbia Journal of Transnational Law* 16 (1971): 392, 397.

23. The convention contains no mention of persons who take part in the conception, preparation, or execution of crimes against diplomats and, under article 3, limits measures applicable under the Convention to "persons . . . charged or convicted for any of the crimes referred to in Article 2 ." By contrast, the draft convention of the Inter-American Juridical Committee had expressly covered co-conspirators and accessories not directly involved in the proscribed acts. Article 5, Inter-American Juridical Committee, draft Convention on Terrorism and Kidnapping of Persons for Extortion, OAS OFF. Records/Ser. G., CP Doc. 54/70 Rev. 1, at 17-22 (1970) (hereinafter cited as Committee Draft Convention).

24. Comment, supra note 22, at 400–401.

25. OAS Convention, supra note 18, art. 2.

26. See the opinion of the Inter-American Juridical Committee accompanying the Committee Draft Convention, supra note 23, at 10 (hereinafter cited as Committee Opinion).

27. Id., at 42.

28. Comment, supra note 22, at 406.

29. For a recent discussion of the European Convention, see Lodge and Freestone, "The European Community and Terrorism: Political and Legal Aspects," in Y. Alexander and K. Myer, eds., *Terrorism in Europe* (1982), p. 79.

30. Invocation of this provision as a ground for refusal of extradition raises a highly sensitive issue, since it imputes bad faith to the request of a state party, which, ex hypothesi, is a friendly state. We shall explore this issue further later in the study.

31. Lodge and Freestone, supra note 29, at 98, fn. 12, report that: "The implications of this provision [article 6] are complex. The United Kingdom implementing legislation, Supression of Terrorism Act, 1978, c. 25, s. 4, extends territorial jurisdiction to the territories of all the contracting states."

32. According to a report, "Treaties and Conventions Relevant to International Terrorism," prepared by Professor Gilliam White (as Special Rapporteur to the International Law Association's Committee on International Terrorism), as of May 1982, Cyprus, Denmark, Ireland, Norway, and Sweden included such a reservation as part of their ratification of the convention. France and Italy made such a reservation upon signing, but neither state has become a party to the convention. See appendix 2, Fourth Interim Report of the Committee on

International Terrorism, *International Law Association Report of the Sixtieth Conference* (1983): 358, 362-63.
33. See Evans, "The Apprehension and Prosecution of Offenders: Some Current Problems," in A. E. Evans and J. F. Murphy, supra note 21, at 498-99.
34. See Lodge and Freestone, supra note 29, at 83.
35. As of May, 1982, only 12 member states of the Council of Europe had ratified the convention.
36. Bull, E. C. 12-1979, point 2.2.68, reprinted in 19 I.L.M. 325 (1980).
37. Dublin Agreement, art. 1.
38. Id., art. 3(1).
39. Id., art. 3(2).
40. Id., art. 6(2).
41. See Lodge and Freestone, supra note 29, at 83.
42. Cuba has agreements with Canada, Mexico, Venezuela, and Colombia; the Soviet Union has agreements with Iran, Finland, and Afghanistan. See Evans, "Aircraft and Aviation Facilities," in A. E. Evans and J. F. Murphy, supra, note 21, at 20, 21, 25.
43. Memorandum of Understanding on Hijacking of Aircraft and Vessels and Other Offenses, entered into force, Feb. 15, 1973, Cuba-United States, 24 U.S.T. 737, T.I.A.S. 7579, reprinted in 12 I.L.M. 370 (1973).
44. United States-Cuba Memorandum, supra note 43, art. 1.
45. Id., art 2.
46. Id.
47. Id., art. 4.
48. See editorial, *Washington Post*, October 19, 1976, at A18, col. 1.
49. See e.g., *New York Times*, Sept. 18, 1980, at A20, col. 1.
50. See, e.g., Convention on Protected Persons, supra note 4, art. 13(1).
51. The Soviet Union and other communist countries, in particular, routinely make such reservations.
52. For an extensive discussion of U.S. and other initiatives in ICAO, see Chamberlain, "Collective Suspension of Air Services with States Which Harbour Hijackers," *International and Comparative Law Quarterly* 32 (1983): 616. The discussion of these initiatives which follows is taken largely from the Chamberlain study.
53. Bonn Declaration on Hijacking of 1978, reprinted in 17 I.L.M. 1285 (1978).
54. For the United States' position, see *American Journal of International Law* 73 (1979): 130. Some German opinion reportedly regards the declaration as binding, but this is a distinctly minority position.
55. As quoted in Chamberlain, supra note 52, at 627.
56. Id.
57. Department of State Bulletin 81 (Aug. 1981): 16.
58. See Chamberlain, supra note 52, at 628.
59. Id.
60. See Philipps, "Die Terrorismus Erklarung des Bonner Weltwirtz—schaftsgipfels aus vollerrechtlicher Sicht," 33 *Juristenzeitung* 33 (1978): 750. For a more positive view of the legality of the Bonn Declaration, see, e.g., Busuttil, "The Bonn Declaration on International Terrorism: A Non-Binding International Agreement on Aircraft Hijacking," *International and Comparative Law Quarterly* 31 (1982): 474.
61. See Chamberlain, supra note 52.
62. Antihijacking Act of 1974, Public Law No. 93-366, 88 Stat. 409 (codified in scattered sections of 49 U.S.C.). The description of the act that follows is taken from Evans, "Aircraft and Aviation Facilities," supra note 42, and the submission of the United States in *The Report of the Secretary-General*, U.N. Doc. A/36/425 (Sept. 21, 1981), at 43.
63. Based on information kindly supplied this writer by the Federal Aviation Administration.
64. Id.
65. The following discussion is based on Murphy, "Protected Persons and Diplomatic Facilities," supra note 21, at 282.
66. The facts of the Lechoco case, as set forth in the following text, are taken from the transcript of sentencing proceedings, which took place on August 22, 1974, before the District

Court for the District of Columbia, the Honorable Howard F. Corcoran presiding (hereinafter cited as "Proceedings"), and from Judge Corcoran's Findings of Fact and Conclusions of Law, dated August 25, 1974. These documents were supplied this writer by Louis G. Fields, then Assistant Legal Adviser for Special Functional Problems, Department of State. Neither of these has been published in the law reports. Upon appeal, in United States v. Lechoco, 542 F.2d 84 (D.C. Cir. 1976), the Circuit Court of Appeals for the District of Columbia reversed and remanded the case to the district court on the ground that it was reversible error for the lower court to exclude proffered testimony relating to defendant's truthfulness during the cross-examination defense and that the issue was crucial to defendant's guilt or innocence. The Circuit Court did not question any of the other findings of fact or conclusions of law made by Judge Corcoran, however.

67. Proceedings, supra note 66, at 10.
68. Id.
69. Id., at 19.
70. 509 F. Supp. 212 (N.D. Cal. 1981), appeal dismissed 622 F.2d 12 (5th Cir. 1980).
71. 284 U.S. 421 (1932).
72. 502 F. Supp. 259 (D.D.C. 1980).
73. Id., at 266.
74. See *Report of the Secretary-General*, supra note 62, at 25.
75. Evans, "Aircraft and Aviation Facilities," in A. E. Evans and J. F. Murphy, eds., *Legal Aspects of International Terrorism* (1978), pp. 3, 15.
76. Murphy, "Protected Persons and Diplomatic Facilities," id. at 277, 282–83.
77. Id., at 284.
78. Id., at 284–85.
79. See note, "Extraterritorial Jurisdiction and Jurisdiction Following Forcible Abduction: A New Israel Precedent in International Law," *Michigan Law Review* 72 (1974): 1087, 1088.

CHAPTER 2

Extradition

Except for the special arrangements discussed in chapter 2, the principle of *aut dedere, aut judicare* does not pertain, since it has not become a rule of customary international law.[1] Moreover, as we have seen, with the exception of the European Convention on the Suppression of Terrorism, the arrangements that have been adopted have taken the "piecemeal" approach and cover only a particular manifestation of international terrorism (attacks on civil aviation or internationally protected persons, hostage taking, and theft of nuclear material). Accordingly, in most instances where a terrorist has committed his actions in one state and flees to another, he will be prosecuted for his crimes only if the country where he is apprehended (requested country) agrees to return him to the country where he committed his crimes (requesting country).

There is general agreement that no rule of customary international law obligates the requested country to return the alleged offender to the requesting country.[2] Rather, such an obligation arises only in situations where the requested country has expressly agreed to do so — usually in the form of an extradition treaty.

These arrangements are often classified as "formal" methods of rendition, rendition being a generic term for the return of alleged offenders to a requesting country. There is no worldwide convention on extradition. Instead, such extradition conventions have been concluded on a regional or bilateral basis, and the two types of arrangements have not been mutually exclusive.

Because the extradition process has often proven to be cumbersome and time-consuming — for reasons we will explore — states have utilized other methods of rendition with greater frequency. These so-called informal methods of rendition, namely, exclusion and deportation, we shall consider in chapter 3.

In this chapter we begin with an overview of regional arrangements for extradition and then explore in some greater detail the European Convention on Extradition and the Inter-American Convention on Extradition. Next we turn to the traditional model of the bilateral extradition treaty as well as to some of the problems that have limited the utility of these arrangements, especially the political offense exception. Finally, we shall analyze, in terms of their significance for efforts to combat international terrorism, some recent developments at the international level and in the United States and selected foreign countries.

Regional Arrangements

OVERVIEW

Regional arrangements for extradition are usually based on geographical proximity or political affinity. In one instance, however—the Scheme Relating to the Rendition of Fugitive Offenders within the Commonwealth[3]—the arrangement can hardly be called regional, and there is little political affinity between some Commonwealth members. Nonetheless, historic ties prompted the Commonwealth members, at a meeting in 1966, while rejecting a multilateral treaty, to agree to the scheme based on reciprocal legislation enacted in each member state in the Commonwealth.[4] The scheme incorporated a number of provisions found in multilateral and bilateral arrangements for extradition, including prohibitions on the extradition of fugitives for political offenses or for the purpose of prosecuting or punishing a fugitive on account of his race, religion, nationality, or political opinion.

A similar scheme was agreed upon by the nordic states. Under the Nordic Treaty of 1962,[5] Denmark, Finland, Iceland, Norway, and Sweden agreed on broad principles of cooperation, including the attainment of "the highest degree of political equality" of all Scandinavian citizens in their territories. Prior to conclusion of this agreement, the nordic states had agreed to a scheme on extradition whereby each state would enact legislation containing similar terms.[6]

Professor Shearer has identified six other "regional" arrangements for extradition, including the Arab League Extradition Agreement, the Benelux Extradition Convention, the European Convention on Extradition, the Inter-American Convention on Extradition, the Convention on Judicial Cooperation of the Organization Communale Africaine at Malgache (OCAM), and the system of bilateral treaties of the Socialist states of Eastern Europe.[7] In this section we limit our examination to a brief review of the European Convention on Extradition and the Inter-American Convention on Extradition.

THE EUROPEAN CONVENTION ON EXTRADITION

The European Convention on Extradition,[8] concluded in 1957, under the auspices of the Council of Europe, had as of May 1982 been ratified by Austria, Cypress, Denmark, Germany, Greece, Ireland, Italy, Liechtenstein, Luxembourg, the Netherlands, Norway, Sweden, Switzerland, and Turkey. Belgium, France, Portugal, and Spain had signed but not ratified the convention. Iceland, Malta, and the United Kingdom alone among the Council of Europe states failed to sign the convention. The convention is also open by invitation to states which are not members of the Council of Europe, and Finland and Israel have acceded through this process.[9]

The primary purpose of the convention is to establish uniform rules with regard to extradition as part of the more general aim of achieving greater unity between member states of the Council of Europe. Limitations on extradition under the convention are substantial. Extradition is not required for political or military offenses, and fiscal offenses are extraditable only if the contracting parties should agree that any particular fiscal offense, or category of offenses, should be covered by the convention. Also, states parties can, in their discretion, refuse to extradite their own nationals. If the offense for which extradition is requested involves the death penalty under the law of the requesting state but not that of the requested state, the latter may refuse extradition unless assurance is given that the death penalty will not be carried out. Requests for provisional arrest may be channeled through the International Criminal Police Organization (Interpol).

It should be noted that the primary purpose of the European Convention on the Suppression of Terrorism, discussed in chapter 1, is to remove the "political offense exception" from applying to certain specified crimes. Accordingly, the political offense exception set forth in the European Convention on Extradition may not apply as between two states parties which are also parties to the European Convention on the Suppression of Terrorism, unless one of the parties has reserved its right under the latter convention to retain the exception in its extradition law and practice.

Two additional protocols to the Convention have been concluded. Accession to these or to any of their articles is open to states which are parties to the European Convention on Extradition but such accession is not obligatory. The first additional protocol, which as of May 1982 had been ratified by three states and signed by four others,[10] includes a limitation on the political offense exception as it applies to war crimes. The second additional protocol is not yet in force, only one ratification having been deposited.[11] It is principally concerned with fiscal offenses and judgments rendered *in absentia*.

INTER-AMERICAN CONVENTION ON EXTRADITION

In the Inter-American region, states have entered into a number of multilateral treaties and conventions relating to extradition.[12] The first was the Montevideo Convention of 1889. The second was a convention concluded in Mexico in 1902, and the third was the Boliviarian Convention concluded at Caracas in 1911. These conventions were followed by the Bustamante Code, adopted in 1928 at Havana by the Sixth International Conference of American States. The provisions of this code were intended to be supplementary only to the provisions of preexisting treaties. The Second Montevideo Convention, concluded in 1933, also did not abrogate preexisting bilateral or collective treaties in force between the parties but automatically was to enter into force in the event of the lapse of prior treaties. Further revisions of the Montevideo Convention took place in 1940 and 1957.

This pattern is continued by the new Inter-American Convention on Extradition, which specifically provides in pertinent part that the convention "shall not supersede multilateral or bilateral treaties that are in force or were concluded earlier unless the States Parties concerned otherwise expressly declare or agree, respectively. . . . The States Parties may decide to maintain in force as supplementary instruments treaties entered into earlier."[13]

The Inter-American Convention on Extradition was adopted by the Organization of American States on February 25, 1981, in Caracas, Venezuela.[14] In its preamble the convention states:

> the close ties and the cooperation that exists in the Americas call for the extension of extradition to ensure that crime does not go unpunished, and to simplify procedures and promote mutual assistance in the field of criminal law on a wider scale than provided for by the treaties in force, with due respect to the human rights embodied in the American Declaration of the Rights and Duties of Man and the Universal Declaration of Human Rights. . . .

To this end the states parties obligate themselves "to surrender to other States Parties that request their extradition persons who are judicially required for prosecution, are being tried, have been convicted or have been sentenced to a penalty involving deprivation of liberty."[15]

Normally, for extradition to be granted, the offense that gave rise to the request for extradition must have been committed in the territory of the requesting state.[16] However, even when the alleged offense has been committed outside the territory of the requesting state, extradition shall be granted if the requesting state has jurisdiction to try the offense and to pronounce judgment thereon.[17]

An extraditable offense is defined under the convention as one that is punishable at the time of its commission by a penalty of not less than two years of deprivation of liberty under the laws of both the requesting and requested states.[18] Under the rule of speciality set forth in the convention, a person extradited "shall not be detained, tried, or punished in the territory of the requesting State for an offense, committed prior to the date of the request for extradition, other than that for which extradition has been granted,"[19] subject to several exceptions including when the "competent authority of the requested state consents to waiver of the rule in the individual case."[20]

The convention sets forth a number of grounds for denying extradition. Most significant among these for present purposes is the political offense exception. Under the convention, extradition cannot be granted

> [w]hen, as determined by the requested State, the offense for which the person is sought is a political offense, an offense related thereto, or an ordinary criminal offense prosecuted for political reasons. The requested state may decide that the fact that the victim of the punishable act in question performed political functions does not in itself justify the designation of the offense as political.[21]

Similarly, the convention provides that no provision of this convention "may be interpreted as a limitation on the right of asylum when its exercise is appropriate."[22] Although the words "when its exercise is appropriate" introduce a measure of ambiguity possibly qualifying its scope, this provision constitutes a major stumbling block to the successful prosecution of international terrorists. Especially in the Americas, efforts to suppress and punish acts of international terrorism have run into problems arising from the complex matrix of asylum, extradition, and the political offense exception. Under the Latin American view, a decision to grant asylum to an accused is necessarily incompatible with the imposition of criminal penalties for offenses committed prior to the grant.[23]

A preferable though hardly ideal approach to limiting the doctrine of asylum's application to international terrorists is found in article 12 of the United Nations Convention on the Prevention and Punishment of Crimes Against Internationally Protected Persons, Including Diplomatic Agents. Article 12 states:

> the provisions of this Convention shall not affect the application of the Treaties on Asylum, in force at the date of the adoption of this Convention, as between states which are parties to those treaties; but a State Party to this Convention may not invoke those Treaties with respect to another State Party to the Convention which is not a party to those Treaties.

The latitude that article 12 gives to the continued application of treaties on asylum among state parties to the convention is carefully circumscribed. It refers only to treaties on asylum in force at the date of the adoption of the convention. Moreover, the article in no way affects the position of states parties that are not also parties to the treaties on asylum. As the United States representative explained to the Sixth (Legal) Committee of the United Nations General Assembly:

> The article states that this Convention shall not affect the application of treaties on asylum in force between parties to those treaties *inter se*. That is to say, even if the alleged offender is present on the territory of one party to such a treaty and the state on the territory of which the crime has taken place is also a party to such a treaty, if the internationally protected person attacked exercised his functions on behalf of a state not party to such a treaty or the alleged offender was a national of a state not party to such a treaty, the state where the alleged offender is present may not invoke that treaty with respect to the non-party state. Thus, the non-party state can hold the state where the alleged offender is present to its obligations under Article 7 [the provision setting forth the extradite or prosecute requirement] and may, if it wishes, request extradition.[24]

Ideally, states in the Americas and elsewhere would adopt the suggestion of the late Alona Evans that prosecution be viewed as an act separate from a grant of political asylum. That is, an alleged offender could be granted asylum in the requested country and still be subject to prosecution in accordance with the usual procedures of that country's criminal process.[25]

The Inter-American Convention on Extradition does contain some provisions that would constitute modest steps forward toward prosecution and punishment of international terrorists. For example, article 5 provides that

> [n]o provision of this Convention shall preclude extradition regulated by a treaty or Convention in force between the requesting State and the requested State whose purpose is to prevent or repress a specific category of offenses and which imposes on such States an obligation to either prosecute or extradite the person sought.

Also, and perhaps more significantly, article 8 states that:

> If, when extradition is applicable, the State does not deliver the person sought, a requested State shall, when its laws or other treaties so permit, be obligated to prosecute him for the offense for which he is charged, just as if it had been committed within its territory, and shall inform the requesting State of the judgment handed down.

Article 8 would be an innovation in extradition law and practice. Usually a requested state, if it declines to extradite, is under no obligation to prosecute even if its laws would permit it. To be sure, unlike the counterterrorist conventions, the Inter-American Convention on Extradition imposes no obligation on states parties to enact legislation permitting them to assume jurisdiction to prosecute an alleged offender apprehended in their territory. Nonetheless, article 8 could stimulate states parties to adopt legislation permitting the exercise on an expansive basis of jurisdiction over terrorist crimes committed outside of their territories and thereby narrow the gap which currently exists between the apprehension, on the one hand, and the prosecution and punishment, on the other, of international terrorists.

Article 21 of the Inter-American Convention provides that a requested state may grant extradition without a formal extradition proceeding, if its laws do not expressly prohibit it and the person sought irrevocably consents in writing to the extradition after being advised by a judge or other competent authority of his right to a formal extradition proceeding and the protection afforded by such a proceeding. Under article 16, the person sought would enjoy in the requested state all the legal rights and guarantees granted by the laws of that state, the assistance of legal counsel, and, if the official language of the country is other than his own, the assistance of an interpreter.

Article 16 would seem an inadequate protection of the rights of an accused because the "legal rights and guarantees" granted by the requested state may be grossly inadequate even to meet minimum standards of human rights. Reference to the rights and legal guarantees contained in the American Declaration of the Rights and Duties of Man and applicable to any person in custody would have been a preferable approach.[26] The American declaration is a counterpart to the Universal Declaration of Human Rights and arguably has attained the status of customary international law. Most states involved in negotiating the Inter-American Convention are signatories to the American declaration (including the United States). In light of the emotional component often present in the prosecution of international terrorists, protection of the fundamental rights of the accused is especially important. The rights and legal guarantees set forth in the American declaration apply both to extradition proceedings and to criminal proceedings. Thus a state party electing not to extradite but to prosecute would be obligated to observe these rules while doing so.

At this writing, the convention has not come into effect. The United States did not sign it and has not yet made a decision on whether to submit it to the Senate for advice and consent to ratification.

Bilateral Extradition Agreements: The Traditional Model

Although, as indicated in the previous section, there are a number of multilateral extradition arrangements, most extradition takes place in accordance with the terms of bilateral extradition treaties. The United States, for example, is a party to extradition treaties with a great variety of states, including such surprises as Albania.[27] Moreover, the United States permits extradition to a requesting state only if it has an extradition treaty with that state.[28] As a matter of policy rather than law, the United States government has declined to utilize the counterterrorist conventions as the basis for extradition, although the terms of these conventions permit such use.

The terms of the particular treaty govern the extradition procedure to be followed. Extradition from the United States is also subject to statutory provisions, which are, as we shall see below, currently under review for possible revision.

Under the traditional model, extradition can take place only if the alleged offender is accused of a crime designated in the treaty. Such treaty lists vary widely and quickly become out-of-date as new crimes are discovered and defined. Moreover, under the doctrine of speciality, these treaties generally require that the accused not be tried for an offense other than that designated in the request for his extradition.

Recently concluded United States extradition treaties have abandoned the list approach and replaced it with a coverage of crimes of a certain level of severity. For example, the extradition treaty between the United States and Costa Rica states in article 2:

Extraditable Offenses

(1) An offense shall be an extraditable offense if it may be punished under the laws of both Contracting Parties by deprivation of liberty for a maximum period of more than one year or by any greater punishment.

(2) An offense shall also be extraditable if it consists of an attempt to commit or participate in the commission of any offense described in paragraph (1) of this Article. Extradition shall also be granted for illicit association, as provided by the law of Costa Rica, to commit any offense described in paragraph (1) of this Article, and for conspiring as provided by the laws of the United States of America, to commit any such offense.

(3) For the purpose of this Article, an offense shall be an extraditable offense:

(a) Whether or not the laws of the Contracting Parties place the offense within the same category of offenses or denominate the offense by the same terminology; or

(b) Whether or not the offense is one for which the United States federal law requires, for the purpose of establishing jurisdiction in a United States federal court, proof of interstate transportation, or use of, or effect on, the mails or other facilities affecting interstate or foreign commerce.

(4) When extradition has been granted for an extraditable offense, it may also be granted for any other offense specified in the request for extradition, even if

the other offense may be punished by less than one year's deprivation of liberty in either State, provided that all other requirements for extradition are met. The Requesting State shall submit the documentation required by Article 9 for each offense for which extradition is requested pursuant to this paragraph.[29]

United States extradition treaties and statutory provisions also provide, *inter alia,* for the issuance of a warrant for the wanted person, for his arrest and commitment, for a public hearing as to the sufficiency of the evidence that his case comes within the terms of the relevant treaty, and for his surrender to agents of the foreign government.

Limitations on the obligation to extradite are many and vary according to the terms of the particular treaty. A general limitation is that extradition "shall be granted only if there is sufficient cause to suspect, according to the laws of the requested party, that the person sought has committed the offense for which extradition is requested or that the person sought is the person convicted by a court of the requesting Party."[30]

Another general limitation in this area is the requirement of "double criminality;" that is, an alleged offender can be extradited only if the acts alleged constitute a crime in both countries. Under some extradition treaties the requirement covers only specific crimes, in which case the principle of *expressio unius* has been held to apply.[31]

The traditional model has allowed extradition only for crimes connected with the requesting state. Some recent treaties — the United States–Japan Extradition Treaty,[32] for example — require extradition even when the offense for which extradition is requested has been committed outside the territory of the requesting party, if the law of the requested party provides for the punishment of such offenses committed outside its territory, or if the offense has been committed by a national of the requesting party.

Other limitations on the obligation to extradite often found in bilateral treaties include a prohibition of extradition of a requested state's nationals; safeguards against double jeopardy; and exclusion of extradition when prosecution of the offense for which extradition is requested would be barred by lapse of time or other reasons under the laws of the requested state. None of these limitations poses problems peculiar to requests for extradition of persons accused of terrorist acts. However, they demonstrate some of the reasons why extradition often proves a cumbersome and time-consuming process for the rendition of international terrorists.

The limitation on extradition most relevant to and obstructive of the rendition of international terrorists is the political offense exception. Typically, an extradition treaty provides that extradition shall *not* be granted when

> the offense for which extradition is requested is a political offense or when it appears that the request for extradition is made with a view to prosecuting,

trying or punishing the person sought for a political offense. If any question arises as to the application of this provision, the decision of the requested Party shall prevail.[33]

As we shall see later in this chapter, more modern United States extradition treaties seek to limit the effect of the political offense exception by specifically excluding certain "terrorist" acts from its scope. Most extradition treaties, however, contain no such provisions; nor do they contain any guidance as to the definition of a political offense. Rather, the courts (most often) or executive branch officials (occasionally) of requested states have the responsibility of interpreting and applying the doctrine to particular situations.

The Political Offense Exception and International Terrorism

We have already examined efforts to deal with the political offense exception through the counterterrorist conventions. It is important to realize, however, that with the exception of the European Convention on the Suppression of Terrorism, none of the counterterrorist conventions limits the discretion of a requested country to invoke the political offense defense in response to a request for extradition. To be sure, under these conventions, if a requested country declines to extradite, it must submit the accused to appropriate national officials for purposes of prosecution. But as we shall see in greater detail below, the process of prosecution under such circumstances itself entails enormous difficulties.

It must also be kept in mind that the global counterterrorist conventions cover only a few of many possible manifestations of terrorism. The European Convention on the Suppression of Terrorism, a regional effort, does attempt to eliminate the political offense exception with respect to terrorist activity, but it has not been effective in doing so. Accordingly, the political offense exception remains a major stumbling block to efforts to prosecute and punish international terrorists.

Like terrorism, the term "political offense" has not been defined by the international community. Moreover, it is probably undefinable. In the words of Sir Hersh Lauterpacht: "Up to the present day, all attempts to formulate a satisfactory conception of the term [political offense] have failed, and the reason of the thing will probably forever exclude the possibility of finding a satisfactory definition."[34]

Dr. Christine Van den Wijngaert has identified three rationales for the political offense exception reflecting in turn three interests involved in the extradition process: those of the accused, the states concerned (requesting and requested state), and international public order.[35] Under the first rationale, the political offense exception has a humanitarian basis and is viewed as protection against an unfair trial in the requesting state which, as the target of the political crime, might be inclined to function as both judge and jury.

The second rationale is based on the principle of neutrality. According to this theory, an inquiry into the extraditability of a political crime would imply a judgment with respect to a political conflict situation in the requesting state. The rendering of such a judgment could in turn amount to the taking of a position with respect to this conflict that would be interpreted as an intervention in the internal affairs of the requesting state. Accordingly, the requested state is well advised to refuse extradition of political offenders *a priori*. Along the same lines, it is contended, "Today's political offenders could be tomorrow's leaders."[36]

Under the third rationale, it is assumed that political crimes do not violate international public order and that states accordingly have no mutual interest in the suppression of such crimes, which have only a local character because they are directed against the domestic public order of the requesting state. Moreover, this rationale holds that international penal cooperation with respect to political offenses is less required than with respect to common offenses because political crimes are less heinous in character. That is, contrary to common crime, political crimes are not inherently "criminal" because the perpetrator acts not according to personal motives but for the benefit of society as a whole.

Dr. Van den Wijngaert has criticized these rationales as follows:

> The reasons advanced in support of the political offense exception are not as logical as they may seem on the surface. Are political offenders always likely to be subject to an unfair and partial trial? Is the nonextradition of political offenders always to be considered as an act of neutrality, or, on the contrary, is it an effective support to political adversaries of the requested state? And finally, is the relative anti-social character of political crimes to be taken for granted?[37]

From an historical perspective, the political offense exception was a late development. Early extradition practice regarded the surrender of political offenders as a primary goal.[38] Sovereigns were directly interested in the suppression of crimes directed against the state and were inclined to pursue prosecutions abroad and collaborate with other sovereigns to ensure that they would be able to prosecute political offenders. As a consequence, political offenders were usually extradited.

Hugo Grotius, although himself a political refugee, accepted the proposition that extradition was granted, in most cases, for crimes against the state, that is, "crimes which affect public order, or which are atrociously criminal."[39] He also contended that states have the duty either to extradite or to punish persons who have committed "crimes by which another state or its sovereign is particularly injured."[40]

A marked change in this anti-political crime attitude took place in the eighteenth century with the rise of revolutionary ideology. This attitude carried over to the nineteenth century and found expression in the Belgian Extradition Act of 1883, the first official codification of the political offense exception.[41] With this act, Belgium adopted the so-called "attentat" clause approach that an attack against the person of a foreign head of state or against the person of a foreign head of state's family member was never to be defined as a political offense. This act also introduced for the first time a limited form of judicial control over extradition. After passage of the act, courts could give advisory opinions on whether an accused was extraditable, although these were not binding and could be rejected by the executive.[42]

Dr. Van den Wijngaert has suggested that, during the eighteenth century, there was a romantic glorification of political offenders.[43] This was based on a "naive" identification of political offenders with the liberal revolutionary. Those supporting this concept did not realize that the political offender might eventually attack the new liberal legal order itself. During the last half of the nineteenth century, the rise of anarchist revolutionaries posed a serious threat to precisely this legal order.

In practice, states have defined the term "political offense" unilaterally, usually through their judiciaries. While doing so, the courts have had little difficulty in concluding that so-called pure political offenses, such as sedition, treason, or unlawful political advocacy should be excluded from extradition. As a consequence, there have been relatively few court cases concerned with pure political offenses.

No such ease of determination has been present with respect to what have come to be called "relative political offenses," under which perpetrators of certain acts that have elements of common crimes, such as killing or infliction of serious bodily injury, were nonetheless deemed worthy of exclusion from the extradition process because their acts were considered political offenses. As to these offenses, there has been little uniformity of approach among the courts in various nations, and this lack of uniformity and consistency has often been present as well in a single jurisdiction.

Dr. Van den Wijngaert has usefully divided attempts to define the relative political offense into the Anglo-Saxon and continental approaches.[44] The Anglo-Saxon approach she titles the "political incidence theory." Under this theory, as developed by British case law, a relative political offense is one committed in the course of a civil war or other political commotion and "incidental to" and part of the political disturbance. Dr. Van den Wijngaert points out that the political incidence theory is an objective approach "since, in principle, only the context of the act, and not the intentions of the perpetrator are taken into consideration."[45] In the early cases of *In re Castioni* (1891)[46] and *In re Meunier* (1894),[47] the British courts were of the opinion that, to establish the political character of an offense, it was necessary to show that it had been committed in the context of a struggle between political parties which were seeking control of the government. Accordingly, in the case of Meunier, an anarchist sought by France on charges of causing explosions, the court concluded that, since anarchists' crimes were committed against all governments rather than against a particular regime, Meunier's acts were not of a political character.

Later British cases, for example *Regina v. Governor of Brixton Prison, ex parte Kolczynski,* took a broader view of the political offense.[48] In *Kolczynski,* the court held that the offense of revolt against the master of a ship on the high seas was committed in order to prevent the offender being prosecuted by an oppressive regime for a political offense (treason in leaving Poland and settling in another country), and that the prospect of such a prosecution gave the offense itself a political character.

In *Regina v. Governor of Brixton Prison, ex parte Schtraks,* Israel requested Schtraks' extradition for having refused to comply with a judicial decision ordering the return of a child to its parents.[49] The Schtraks family refused to return the child on the ground that it would no longer have a strict orthodox education with its parents. The case gave rise to considerable controversy in Israel between left-wing liberal and right-wing orthodox Jews. Because of this, Schtraks argued in Great Britain that his act was a political offense. The Queens Bench rejected this argument on the ground that the political conflict developed only *after* Schtraks' act. On appeal the House of Lords affirmed but on a different ground. The Lords agreed that this was a political conflict situation, but emphasized that the Israeli government had taken a neutral stand with respect to the conflict. There was no conflict, therefore, between Schtraks and the Israeli government as required by the political offense doctrine.

Debate in the House of Lords with respect to the Schtraks case and judgments rendered in that case bear importantly on the scope of the political offense doctrine under British law. As stated by Lord Reid:

> We cannot inquire whether a fugitive criminal was engaged in a good or bad cause . . . but not every person who commits an offense in the course of a political struggle is entitled to protection . . . so it appears to me that the motive and purpose of the accused in committing the offense must be relevant and must be decisive and I do not see why the section should be limited to attempts to overthrow a government. The use of force, or it may be of other means, to compel a sovereign to change his advisors, or to compel a government to change its policy may be just as political in character as the use of force to achieve a revolution.[50]

Viscount Radcliffe added to Lord Reid's comments the following:

> In my opinion the idea that lies behind the phrase "offense of a political character" is that the fugitive is at odds with the State that applied for his extradi-

tion on some issue connected with the political control or government of the country. The analogy of political in this context is with political in such phrases as political refugee, political asylum, or political prisoner. It does indicate, I think, that the requesting State is after him for reasons other than the enforcement of the criminal law in its ordinary, what I may call its common international aspect.

. . . It is still necessary to maintain the idea of that connection [connecting the political offense with an uprising, a disturbance, an insurrection, a civil war or struggle for power]. It is not departed from by taking a liberal view as to what is meant by disturbance or these other words, provided that the idea of political opposition as between fugitive and requesting State is not lost sight of; but it would be lost sight of, I think, if one were to say that all offenses were political offenses, so long as they could be shown to have been committed for a political object or with a political motive or for the furtherance of some political cause or campaign.[51]

The case of *Regina v. Governor of Pentonville Prison, ex parte Tzu-Tsai Cheng* added a new twist to the British version of the political incidence theory.[52] There, the fugitive had been convicted of attempted murder in New York, but his offense was directed against the government of a third state (Taiwan). The majority of the court held that this did not constitute a political offense because it was not directed against the government of the state in which it was committed (the United States) and which was seeking the offender's extradition.

As summarized by Dr. Van den Wijngaert:

The British practice shows a relatively consistent application of its original criterion, the political incidence test. Nonetheless, there seems to be a tendency to de-emphasize its strict application and to supplement it with other criteria. The rationale of the political offense exception is not overlooked, the rule being applied in a broader . . . or in a narrower . . . manner according to whether the refugee is or is not "at odds" with the state requesting his extradition. Normally, requirements for such a relationship (at odds) are only fulfilled if the requesting state is, at the same time the target state of the political offense. . . . Reading between the lines of the different decisions, a gradual evolution towards increased emphasis on subjective criteria can be noted. . . . The lacuna in the British approach, however, is that too little attention is being paid to the act itself. In other words, the seriousness or the international character of the act does not directly affect its liability to extradition.[53]

Dr. Van den Wijngaert has charged that United States case law "has not known the same flexible development as the British and is still strongly anchored to the strict nineteenth century criteria of *Castioni* and *Meunier*."[54] As evidence, she cites, *inter alia,* the *Jimenez* and *Gonzales* decisions. In *Jimenez v. Aristeguieta, et al.,*[55] Venezuela demanded the extradition of its ex-president, Jimenez, who had been overthrown by a coup d'état. The crimes he allegedly committed during his presidency included murder, attempted murder, and financial corruption. With respect to the alleged murder and attempted murder, the court found the facts insufficiently proven to support a finding of probable cause. But Jimenez was found extraditable on the basis of the financial crimes, which did not qualify as political offenses because there was "no evidence that the financial crimes charged were committed in the course of and incidentally to a revolutionary uprising or other violent political disturbance."[56] The slim chance of Jimenez receiving a fair trial by those who had violently overthrown his government seemed to have escaped the court's notice.

The government of the Dominican Republic in *In re Gonzales*[57] requested the extradition of one of its nationals charged with murder and torture of political prisoners under the former regime of Rafael Trujillo. The alleged crimes had been committed by Gonzales in a military or quasi-military capacity. The court declined to characterize these crimes as political because, at the moment of their commission, there was no political uprising to which they were incidental. In Dr. Van den Wijngaert's opinion:

> The *Gonzales* case illustrates the weakness of the political incidence theory. With respect to extremely serious crimes such as the alleged torturing and killing of political prisoners as in that case, the pure political incidence test is too formalistic and, in addition, incomplete. Due attention should have been paid to the seriousness of the acts, rather than to the question of whether they were incidental to and part of a political conflict situation. In this respect the political incidence theory is incomplete and thus unsatisfactory.[58]

Dr. Van den Wijngaert also cites the *Artukovic* case as a "flagrant example" of the deficiencies of a pure political incidence approach.[59] As minister of the interior of the pro-Hitler Pavelic government in Croatia during the war, Artukovic had been responsible for the killings of thousands of Jews, Serbs, and Gypsies. Both the federal district court and the court of appeals accepted Artukovic's argument that his crimes were political on the ground that they were incidental to the political conflict of World War II. Neither the seriousness nor the international character of the war crimes and genocide charged to Artukovic were taken into account. These courts also dismissed United Nations resolutions unequivocally recommending the extradition of war criminals as having no binding legal effect.

Five recent cases illustrate that the approach of United States courts has changed little. In *In re McMullen*,[60] the alleged offender was a deserter from the British army who had joined the Provisional Wing of the Irish Republic Army (PIRA). He was charged with participating in the bombing of the Claro Barracks in Great Britain, which resulted in the death of a charwoman. When he was apprehended in the United States, Great Britain sought his extradition pursuant to the provisions of the United States-

United Kingdom Extradition Treaty which includes the standard exception for political offenses. At his hearing, McMullin alleged that Great Britain was seeking his extradition for a political offense. The magistrate agreed. In so ruling he found that "an insurrection and a disruptive uprising of a political nature did, in fact, existed [sic] in Northern Ireland in 1970 and particularly in 1974, when Mr. McMullin is charged with the crimes against Claro Barracks, a British Army installation" and that McMullin had "acted as a member of PIRA. His activities were directed by . . . the PIRA and . . . the bombing was a crime incidental to and formed part of a political disturbance, uprising or insurrection and in furtherance thereof."[61]

In contrast, the magistrate rejected the defense of a political exception in the *Abu Eain* case.[62] Mr. Eain was alleged to have killed two young Jewish males and wounded 36 others by the delayed detonation of an explosive device placed in a trash bin in a public market place in Tiberius, Israel, on May 14, 1979. After Mr. Eain was apprehended in Chicago, Israel sought his extradition under the United States-Israel Extradition Treaty. In rejecting Mr. Eain's argument that his acts constituted a political offense, the magistrate stated the

> random and indiscriminate placing of an explosive near a bus stop on a public street in a trash bin diffuses any theory that the target was a military one or justified by any military necessity. . . . The commission of these alleged offenses is so remote from the political objective that it could not reasonably have been believed by the offender to have a direct political effect on the government of Israel; nor was it directed at the government of Israel.[63]

Eain's petition for a writ of habeas corpus was denied by the United States District Court for the Northern District of Illinois, and that court's denial was upheld by the United States Court of Appeals for the Seventh Circuit.[64]

The United States magistrate for the Southern District of New York, in *In re Mackin*,[65] took 101 pages to determine that Mr. Mackin's alleged shooting of a British policeman in Northern Ireland constituted a political offense within the meaning of the United States–United Kingdom Extradition Treaty, and that his extradition was therefore barred. The government sought to convince the United States Court of Appeals for the Second Circuit that it had jurisdiction to review the magistrate's decision, but the court declined to accept the appeal.[66]

Similarly, on October 3, 1983, the United States District Court for the Northern District of California ordered the release from jail of William Joseph Quinn, an alleged Irish Republic Army member accused of shooting a London police constable to death in 1975 and of conspiring to send letter bombs to a Catholic bishop, a British judge and a newspaper executive.[67] Explosives were placed at a railroad station and two restaurants; two of the bombs exploded, causing serious injuries. The court ruled that all of these alleged crimes constituted political offenses.

In light of previous United States decisions, and their adoption of the political incidence test, the court's classification of Quinn's shooting of a British police constable as a political offense was arguably correct. However, the court was almost surely mistaken in similarly classifying as political offenses Quinn's sending of letter bombs and his involvement in the planting of bombs. Even during times of armed conflict governed by the laws of war, the deliberate targetting of civilians constitutes a crime subject to prosecution and punishment. That the violence directed against the general civilian population was incidental "to the political goals of seeking an end to British rule in Northern Ireland," a factor cited by the court in support of its decision, would not excuse a crime under the law of armed conflict. Indeed, the decision in *Quinn* seems clearly inconsistent with the ruling in *Abu Eain*.

Most recently, in this line of cases involving members of the Provisional Irish Republican Army, John E. Sprizzo, District Judge for the Southern District of New York, denied a request to extradite Joseph Patrick Thomas Doherty to the United Kingdom.[68] Mr. Doherty did not deny that he had been involved in a PIRA attack in Northern Ireland on a convoy of British soldiers; that this attack resulted in the death of a British soldier; that he had been arrested, charged with murder, among other crimes, and held in a prison in Northern Ireland pending trial; that after trial was completed but before any decision by the court, he escaped from the prison; that he was convicted in absentia of murder, attempted murder, illegal possession of firearms and ammunition, and belonging to the Irish Republican Army; and that following his arrest in New York City, the British government had filed a formal request for his extradition on August 16, 1983. Doherty claimed, however, that his extradition should be denied on the ground that the offenses for which extradition was requested constituted political offenses.

The District Court upheld Mr. Doherty's contention. In Judge Sprizzo's view,

> the facts of this case present the assertion of the political offense exception in its most classic form. The death of Captain Westnacott, while a most tragic event, occurred in the context of an attempted ambush of a British army patrol. It was the British army's response to that action that gave rise to Captain Westnacott's death. Had this conduct occurred during the course of more traditional military hostilities, there could be little doubt that it would fall within the political offense exception.[69]

Judge Sprizzo went on to hold that, while "it would be most unusual as a matter of policy to extend the benefit of the political offense exception to every fanatic group or individual with loosely defined political objectives who commit acts of violence in the name of those so-called political objectives," the PIRA has "an organization, discipline, and command structure that distinguishes it from more amorphous groups such as the Black Liberation Army or the Red Brigade."[70] Moreover, Judge Sprizzo declined to "make the political exception concept turn upon the Court's assessment of the likelihood of a movement's success. History is replete with examples of political and insurrectionary movements that have succeeded in effecting political changes that were believed to be improbable if not impossible."[71]

It is interesting that by way of dicta, Judge Sprizzo distinguished Doherty's case from situations where the political offense exception would not apply. For example, he noted that the court was not faced with a situation "in which a bomb was detonated in a department store, public tavern, or a resort hotel, causing indiscriminate personal injury, death, and property damage." Nor was it "a case where violence was directed against civilian representatives of the government, where defining the limits of the political offense exception would be far less clear;" or "a case where the alleged political conduct was committed in a place other than the territory where political change was to be effected, a circumstance that would in all probability render the political offense exception inapplicable." Finally, the court was "not presented with facts which establish that hostages were killed or injured or where the principles embodied in the Geneva Convention have clearly been violated."[72]

According to Dr. Van den Wijngaert, there is no single theoretical approach to the problem of the finding of political crimes among the countries on the Continent: "Except for the fact that a stronger emphasis is laid on subjective elements, the courts on 'the Continent' have used a great variety of criteria."[73] Nonetheless, Dr. Van den Wijngaert has suggested that the approach followed on the Continent can be roughly classified into objective, subjective, and mixed theories. The pure objective theory, which takes no account of the motives of the perpetrator, is seldom applied today. The subjective approach, however, does have substantial support in some countries. For example, although they have not been consistent in this regard, French courts have often focused on the subjective rather than on the objective theory. That is, to determine whether a given offense is of a political or common character, the French courts have inquired whether the perpetrator has acted with a political motive or for a political purpose.

An egregious example of this approach was the *Holder-Kerkow* case in which several American nationals hijacked an airplane and made vague allusions to Angela Davis and against the Vietnam War while extorting $500,000 from the aircraft company.[74] In response to a request from the United States government for their extradition, the French Court of Appeals ruled that the hijacking was a political crime because the motives of the perpetrators were of a political nature.

More recently, the French courts have shifted their emphasis away from the motives of the perpetrator. For example, in the *Klaus Croissant* case, the

Federal Republic of Germany requested the extradition of an attorney who had had several members of the Baader-Meinhoff gang as clients.[75] Croissant was accused of (a) forming a net of communications for the benefit of a criminal organization, and (b) granting indirect assistance to a criminal organization, including the organization of hunger strikes and the carrying on of an intense propaganda campaign for the group. In rejecting Croissant's claim that these acts were political crimes, the Court of Appeals of Paris reformulated the French approach to the effect that the "gravity" of the offenses—that is, their "odious" criminal character—precluded a consideration of the political motivation.

Similarly, in 1979, Italy requested the extradition of one Piperno on the ground that he had participated in the kidnapping and murder of Prime Minister Aldo Moro in the spring of 1978. Again, the Court of Appeals of Paris rejected the claim that the accused's alleged offense was of a political character:

> But the count reveals the extreme seriousness of the facts alleged since, in addition to the physical and mental torture implied by sequestration of many weeks, they have consisted of the killing of the innocent hostage. Whatever be the purpose pursued or the context in which such acts are located, they cannot, taking into account their seriousness, be considered as being of a political character.[76]

Professor Thomas Carbonneau has summarized the current French theoretical position and explained the inconsistency of French court decisions as follows:

> The proverbial black letter of French jurisprudence on the political offense exception can be summarized as follows. Terrorist acts are criminal acts, and their grave criminal character precludes any consideration of their underlying political motivation for purposes of extradition. Even when the acts are not sufficiently grave or odious, terrorist activities are not quintessentially political crimes, but rather are akin to anarchistic activities—a social crime for which extradition will lie. This position appears to be the constant doctrine of the French courts when they function as neutral arbiters of disputes; it is a stance which merits study and imitation by the courts of other countries.
>
> The influence of external political circumstances has detracted considerably from the elaboration of this doctrine in certain cases—such as *Holder, Abu Daoud,* and the Spanish cases. It is extremely unfortunate that the French judiciary acquiesced to the dictates of executive branch policies or willingly gave voice to them in its determinations through unreasoned pronouncements or by resort to artificially technical analysis.[77]

Dr. Van den Wijngaert has noted with respect to the mixed approach that while it avoids some of the drawbacks of the purely objective and subjective theories, it should nonetheless be noted that there is one element which is completely left out of consideration in the subjective, objective and thus also mixed theories: the treatment to which the requested person is to be subjected in the requesting state.[78]

Although the British courts have, in the more recent cases, tended to focus on this element, this has not been true of United States courts, where the rule of non-inquiry has precluded such an examination. To be sure, at least in theory this factor is considered by the executive branch, which has the final decision on extradition. In practice its effect as a limitation on extradition is at best problematic.

For her part, Dr. Van den Wijngaert has written favorably of an approach taken by the Swiss: the proportionality theory, also referred to as the predominance or preponderance theory.[79] Under this approach, a crime will qualify for the political offense exception only if it is *predominantly political*—that is, if the political element outweighs the common element. Article 10 of the Swiss Extradition Act provides that extradition is permitted "even if the guilty person alleges a political motive or end, if the act for which it has been requested constitutes primarily a common offense."[80] Article 3, paragraph 2, of the Swiss act also expressly excludes an act from the political offense exception if it

> (a) was aimed at the extermination or oppression of a segment of the population on account of nationality, race, religion, or ethnic, social or political affiliation; or
>
> (b) appears particularly reprehensible because the offender, for the purpose of extortion or duress, placed or threatened to place under jeopardy the freedom, life or limb of persons, especially by hijacking planes, taking hostages or using means of mass extermination.

The Austrian Extradition Act also adopts the proportionalty test and excepts politically motivated offenses from extradition unless the criminal character outweighs the political one under consideration of all the circumstances of the case.[81] The criteria employed by the Austrian courts for determining whether an act is a political offense focus on the mode of perpetration, the means employed, and the seriousness of the intended or resulting consequences.[82] As applied, these criteria have generally ruled out classifying acts of international terrorism as political crimes. For example, in a 1968 case, an Austrian court found that the seriousness of the offense—the killing of several persons by explosives—outweighed the political motive. Nonetheless, extradition was denied because of a concern that the offender would be subject to persecution.[83] Under section 19 of the Austrian act, extradition is disallowed if there is reason to fear that the fugitive would be subjected to persecution in the requested state for religious, political, or ethnic reasons. At the same time, the Austrian act provides that, if extradition is refused because of the danger of persecution in the requesting state, the alleged offender may be submitted to prosecution in Austria for the crime. Thus, in one case a fugitive from Hungary who had committed a homicide in the course of his flight was granted political asylum upon arrival in Austria.[84] Extradition to Hungary was refused for various reasons, among them the danger of persecution. However, the alleged offender was tried in Austria because the crime did not qualify as a political offense, since the seriousness of the act outweighed the political motive of the flight.

Dr. Van den Wijngaert has supported the proportionality theory in the following terms:

> As an argument in favour of the proportionality theory, it can be noted that, much more than the political incidence theory and the subjective and objective theories, at least in a much more explicit manner, the proportionality theory takes into account the seriousness of the act by relating it to the political purpose sought after. Whereas the determination of the political or common character of a crime is always arguable, the determination of its seriousness is much less liable to discussion. Here lies, in this writer's opinion, the relative objectivity of the proportionality theory. . . .
>
> Elements such as the seriousness of the act, the proportionality between act and purpose, the absence of political motives, etc. directly prevail in the determination of the extraditability of the act, rather than abstract considerations with respect to the nature of the act; the emphasis is laid upon the act itself and both the intentions behind it and its consequences are evaluated in function of it. For these reasons, the proportionality theory is, in this writer's opinion, to be preferred above the other theories.[85]

Recent Developments Regarding Extradition, the Political Offense Exception, and International Terrorism

INTERNATIONAL

As noted above, the only international development directly involving states that attempts to cope with the problems of extradition, the political offense exception and international terrorism has been the European Convention on the Suppression of Terrorism. Recently, however, the Committee on International Terrorism of the International Law Association, a nongovernment group of international law scholars and practitioners, has made a number of proposals that may have substantial impact on efforts to combat international terrorism in general and on the problem of the political offense exception in particular.[86]

Specifically, the committee has proposed, in the form of a resolution to the sixty-first conference of the International Law Association, a working definition of international terrorism, principles, and statements of applicable rules of law that come into play as a result of terrorist actions. Part II of the Committee's report, which includes the operative text and explanations, is set forth in full below.

Part II. Operative Text and Explanations

1. *Statement of Principle*
Certain acts are so reprehensible that they are of concern to the international community, whether they are perpetrated in time of peace or war, irrespective of the justice of the cause which the perpetrators pursue, and regardless of political motivation. All such acts must be suppressed.

EXPLANATION. This statement is derived from Principle I of the Principles of International Law Recognized in the Charter and Judgment of the Nuremberg Tribunal, adopted by the United Nations General Assembly in 1950 (U.N. G.A.O.R., 5th session, supp. no. 12, Doc. A/1316, p. 11). That Principle applies to crimes against the peace and crimes against humanity as well as the more traditional war crimes. It is suggested that the underlying principle, stated here, is applicable even more broadly.

2. *Working Definition*
The acts referred to in the Statement of Principle include acts defined as offenses of international significance in treaties as well as acts of international terrorism. Acts of international terrorism include but are not limited to atrocities, wanton killing, hostage taking, hijacking, extortion, or torture committed or threatened to be committed whether in peacetime or in wartime for political purposes provided that an international element is involved. An act of terrorism is deemed to have an international element when the offense is committed within the jurisdiction of one country:

(a) against any foreign government or international organization, or any representative thereof; or

(b) against any national of a foreign country because he is a national of a foreign country; or

(c) by a person who crosses an international frontier into another country from which his extradition is requested.

EXPLANATION. To be classified as "international terrorism" for the purposes of applying the rules of law set out here, an act must be so reprehensible or so disruptive of the fabric of society that no motivation or political subordination can excuse it. The acts listed here as illustrative include acts which violate all known municipal criminal law codes and which, if done in wartime, would seem to be violations of the laws of war. In the absence of an international element, all these acts are properly handled by each state for itself. When an international element is involved, the suppression of these and similar acts becomes a matter of international concern. Three situations are envisaged in which the international element must be deemed to exist.

3. *Combatant Status No Exculpation*

(a) The claim of combatant status does not legitimize an act of international terrorism.

(b) No state may permit a person to escape trial or extradition for an act of international terrorism, on the ground that that person should be regarded as a combatant, if the act is illegal under the laws of armed conflict.

EXPLANATION. As noted in the Working Definition, the acts of international terrorism are qualified as such whether committed in peacetime or wartime. Thus attempts to avoid the legal results of committing such offenses should be rejected when those attempts are based upon the claim of combatant status or the claim that the acts constitute a "mere" war crime rather than international terrorism.

4. *Political Motivation No Exculpation*

No state may legally permit a person who has committed an act of international terrorism to escape trial or extradition on the ground of his political motivation.

EXPLANATION. The legal obligation of a state to try or extradite some persons regardless of their political motivations already exists in the case of some offenses, such as aircraft hijacking, where the usual political offense exception to bilateral extradition treaties has been felt to be inappropriate. The Committee concluded that international terrorism as defined above requires similar handling by states.

5. *International Competence over Individuals*

Acts of international terrorism, no less than crimes against humanity, are violations of international law by individuals regardless of motivation or political context.

EXPLANATION. Principle VI of the Principles of International Law Recognized in the Charter and Judgment of the Nuremberg Tribunal defines crimes against humanity to include various reprehensible acts only when carried on in execution of or in connection with a crime against the peace or war crime. It seems to be part of the progressive development of the conscience of mankind in peacetime to accept international concern over the identical acts and others added by international consensus and practice to the class "crimes against humanity," bearing the same legal consequences for individual perpetrators. The acts listed as illustrative in the Working Definition above would seem to fall into that category regardless of whether the status of war or of peace is considered to govern.

6. *Superior Orders No Defence*

The official position of an accused or the existence of superior orders is no defence to a person accused of an act of international terrorism.

EXPLANATION. Individual responsibility and the ineffectiveness of the plea of superior orders when moral choice is in fact possible are stated in Principles

III and IV of the Principles of International Law Recognized in the Charter and Judgment of the Nuremberg Tribunal. The Committee concluded that the same principles were applicable to cases of international terrorism as defined above for purposes of this statement of rules of law.

7. *Aut Judicare Aut Dedere*

States must try or extradite (*aut judicare aut dedere*) persons accused of acts of international terrorism. No state may refuse to try or extradite a person accused of an act of international terrorism, war crime, common crime which would be a war crime but for the absence of a legal status of belligerency, or a crime against humanity, on the basis of disagreement as to which of these legal categories properly applies to the situation.

EXPLANATION. A fundamental legal principle requires that an accused be informed of the charges against him and be given an opportunity to respond. That principle applies both to cases of trial within a single country and to extradition from one country to another. Awkward situations can arise when, in an extradition proceeding, the state requesting extradition and the state with custody of the accused differ as to the legal qualification of the facts, even when there is no dispute as to fact and the different qualifications lead to the same result. The rule stated here as corollary to the basic obligation to try or extradite (*aut judicare aut dedere*) does not require that states agree on the precise category in which to classify the acts, but leaves to the individual states concerned the decision as to how best to interpret a particular extradition agreement to avoid a failure of the enforcement system of the law. As long as the accused is fully informed of the facts on the basis of which his trial or extradition is sought, and the legal consequences to him if those facts are proved in the appropriate way before the appropriate tribunal, no violation of that fundamental principle can be involved. The problem is a routine problem of extradition between states whose criminal codes and procedures differ, and should not be regarded as posing extraordinary obstacles in the case of particularly reprehensible acts of international concern, international terrorism.

8. *State Support for International Terrorism Forbidden*

No state may afford support to a person or group engaged or preparing to engage in acts of international terrorism.

EXPLANATION. In some cases, support for acts which might be regarded as acts of international terrorism could be considered aggression under the United Nations General Assembly's consensus definition of April 1974 (U.N. Doc. A/Ac. 134/1.46, articles 3(f) and (g)). In other cases, such support might be an interference in the internal affairs of another state. No situation could be envisaged in which state support for persons or groups engaged or preparing to engage in the acts included above in the Working Definition of international terrorism would not violate basic rules of international law.

9. *Due Diligence Required*

A state is legally obliged to exercise due diligence to prevent the commission of acts of international terrorism within its jurisdiction.

EXPLANATION. This statement codifies a basic principle of international tort liability. Its applicability to international terrorism has been convincingly argued in Lillich & Paxman, "State Responsibility for Injuries to Aliens Occasioned by Terrorist Activities," 26 American University Law Review 219 (1977).

10. *International Communication and Transportation of Universal Legal Concern*
Acts of international terrorism directed against the means of international transportation which by treaty or international practice are open to international traffic, are of legal interest to all states. No state may legally refuse to participate in measures to safeguard those means from acts of international terrorism on the ground of lack of legal interest.

EXPLANATION. This statement expresses the special interest of the international community in protecting the means of international communication and transportation partially evidenced in the wide adoption of the Tokyo Convention on Offenses and Certain Other Ats Committed on Board Aircraft, 14 September 1963, 704 U.N.T.S. 219; the Hague Convention on the Suppression of Unlawful Seizure of Aircraft, 16 December 1970, 860 U.N.T.S. 105; the Montreal Convention for the Suppression of Unlawful Acts Against the Safety of Civil Aviation, 23 September 1971, 24 U.S.J. 564, U.K.T.S. No. 10 (1974); and the Lausanne Protocol of 5 July 1974, which was the second additional protocol to the Vienna Constitution of the Universal Postal Union dated 10 July 1964. The importance of stating the legal interest of all states in measures to safeguard those means from international terrorism flows from the restrictive view of legal interest taken by the International Court of Justice in the *South West Africa Cases, Second Phase* [1966] I.C.J. 6.

11. *Organs of Communication and Diplomatic and Consular Establishments of Universal Legal Concern*
Acts of international terrorism directed against official organs of communication, including diplomatic and consular establishments, special missions, and the people engaged in maintaining them, are of legal interest to all states. No state may legally refuse to participate in measures to safeguard those organs and people from acts of international terrorism on the ground of lack of legal interest.

EXPLANATION. This statement expresses the special interest of the international community in protecting official organs of communication such as those the subject of the United National Convention on the Prevention and Punishment of Crimes Against Internationally Protected Persons, Including Diplomatic Agents, dated 14 December 1973. The importance of stating the legal interest of all states in measures to safeguard those organs from international terrorism flows from the restrictive view of legal interest taken by the International Court of Justice in the *South West Africa Cases, Second Phase* [1966] I.C.J. 6.

12. *Specially Dangerous or Poisonous Materials of Universal Legal Concern*
Acts of international terrorism involving the possession, diverson or use of specially dangerous or poisonous materials contrary to applicable national law or treaty, particularly nuclear materials, psychotropic drugs, and any materials made the subject of the 1972 Convention on the Development, Pro-

duction and Stockpiling of Bacterological (Biological) and Toxin Weapons and on their Destruction, are of legal concern to all states. No state may refuse to participate in measures to safeguard such materials on the ground of lack of legal interest.

EXPLANATION. This statement expresses the special interest of the international community in protecting specially dangerous materials from diversion to the use of international terrorists. It incorporates the principles that underlie the 1972 Convention cited in its text, the IAEA Convention on the Physical Protection of Nuclear Material dated 26 October 1979, 18 International Legal Materials 1419 (1979), and various conventions and agreements relating to control of the international traffic in narcotic drugs. The concern of this rule is not the enforcement of municipal law as such, but with keeping specially dangerous substances and poisons out of the armoury of international terrorism. Thus, it is important to state the legal interest of all states in the matter.

13. *State Responsibility*
Breach of any of these rules entails state responsibility.

EXPLANATION. It seems important to the Committee that the responsiblity of states be engaged directly in the enforcement of the rules set forth above. Mere statements of rules with no provisions for who is responsible to enforce them would be an empty gesture.

14. *Continuity of General Legal Obligations*
The existence of international agreements under which rules parallel to these are enunciated, or specific obligations undertaken by the parties to take action to implement some of these obligations, does not imply the weakening of any obligations resting on general international law either for the parties to any of these agreements or for non-parties, unless specifically so provided among the parties in such an agreement.

EXPLANATION. General obligations owed to the international community cannot be discharged by accepting specific obligations only to some members of that community. The problem of international terrorism appears serious enough to the international community as a whole that it seems appropriate to restate the continued existence of the general obligation regardless of specific agreements that deal with parts of it.

The part of the committee's report excerpted above contains a number of claims of law that, if widely accepted by states, would represent a major step forward in the effort to apprehend, prosecute and punish international terrorists. Sections 3, 4, 5, and 6, for example, seek to close any gap that may exist between the law relating to terrorism in armed conflict and that applicable to terrorism occurring during peacetime. Individual terrorists, sometimes supported by states, have often claimed combatant status or their political motivation as a defense to extradition or prosecution. Such claims have been categorically rejected by the committee.

Section 5 of Part II of the committee's report supports the important proposition that acts of international terrorism are international crimes subject to the universality principle of criminal jurisdiction. Section 5 should be read in conjunction with section 7, which sets forth the debatable proposition that states must try or extradite persons accused of acts of international terrorism. Section 7's proposition is debatable because the extradite or prosecute requirement has to date been *expressly* accepted by the world community, in the form of conventions, only with respect to particular manifestations of international terrorism — that is, attack on civil aviation or internationally protected persons, hostage taking, and the theft of nuclear materials. Accordingly, section 7 may represent a claim *de lege feranda*. Acceptance of the committee's claim by member states of the world community and its resultant establishment as a norm of customary international law would be a truly revolutionary but highly helpful development.

Sections 10, 11, and 12 of Part II of the committee's report expand upon article 2(6) of the United Nations Charter, which enjoins the organization to ensure that states which are not members act in accordance with United Nations principles so far as may be necessary for the maintenance of international peace and security. They are innovative in that they set forth the debatable proposition that the *lex lata* requires states not parties to the listed counterterrorist conventions to cooperate in their implementation. Widespread acceptance of this proposition by member states of the world community would lend a substantial measure of support to efforts like the Bonn Declaration to deal with states that offer safe haven or other assistance to international terrorists.

The report of the Committee was approved by the International Law Association in September, 1984, at the ILA's sixty-first conference in Paris. What influence the approach it espouses will have on states remains to be seen. One would hope, however, that at a minimum, sections 3, 4, 5, and 7 of the report, discussed above, will gain widespread acceptance. No matter how just the cause or how pure the political motivation of an accused, all states should agree to extradite or try all persons who commit acts that would be characterized as war crimes, or as crimes against humanity, but for the absence of legal status of belligerency. Minimal dictates of humanity and justice require no less.

THE UNITED STATES

As noted above in the section on the political offense exception and international terrorism, the United States government reacted strongly to the magistrates' decisions in the *McMullen* and *Mackin* cases that IRA members had committed political offenses by bombing British military barracks in England and shooting a British policeman in Northern Ireland. Having failed to convince the courts that the current law reserved the decision on the political offense exception to the executive branch, the government sought to accomplish such a reservation by including in newly concluded bilateral extradition treaties specific provisions reserving to the "Executive authority of the requested party"[87] the power to determine whether an offense for which extradition is requested falls within the political offense exception. More generally, the executive branch prompted introduction of a bill in the Senate that would, *inter alia,* have granted both the government and the accused the right to appeal a district court or magistrate decision, on various issues of extradition law, but reserve to the sole discretion of the secretary of state the decision whether the political offense exception is applicable.[88]

Senate hearings on the bill revealed general agreement on the provision granting both the government and the accused the right of appeal, as well as on a number of other changes in current extradition law that would be effected by the draft legislation.[89] There was, however, substantial opposition to transferring the decision-making authority from the courts to the secretary of state. It was argued that exclusion of the judiciary from the decision-making process would undermine the purpose of the political offense doctrine to protect individuals from government oppression and subject the doctrine to the political calculations of governments.[90]

These and other arguments prevailed, and later bills introduced in Congress have retained for the courts the decision-making authority on the political offense exception. At this writing, none of these bills has yet been adopted by Congress. Nonetheless, it may be instructive for us to consider and compare some of the bills introduced in the Senate and the House as they attempt to deal with the political offense exception and international terrorism. First, we consider the approach taken by the Senate in the Comprehensive Crime Control Act of 1983 (S. 1972, 97th Cong.). On October 5, 1984, part M of Title X of the Comprehensive Control Act of 1984 relating to international extradition was dropped from the act in response to a filibuster threat. Section 3194(e) of S. 1972 provides:

> (e) POLITICAL OFFENSES AND OFFENSES OF A POLITICAL CHARACTER — The court shall not find the person extraditable after a hearing under this section if the court finds that the person has established by clear and convincing evidence that any offense for which such person may be subject to prosecution or punishment if extradited is a political offense or an offense of a political character. For the purposes of this subsection, the terms "political offense" and "offense of a political character" —
>
> (1) do not include —
>
> > (A) an offense within the scope of the Convention for the Suppression of Unilateral Seizure of Aircraft, signed at the Hague on December 16, 1970;
> >
> > (B) an offense within the scope of the Convention for the Suppression of Unlawful Acts Against the Safety of Civil Aviation, signed at Montreal on September 23, 1971;

(C) a serious offense involving an attack against the life, physical integrity, or liberty of an internationally protected person (as defined in section 1116 of this title), including a diplomatic agent;

(D) an offense with respect to which a multilateral treaty obligates the United States to either extradite or submit for the purposes of prosecution a person accused of the offense;

(E) an offense that consists of the manufacture, importation, distribution, or sale of narcotics or dangerous drugs;

(F) an offense that consists of forceable sexual assault;

(G) an attempt or conspiracy to commit an offense described in subparagraphs (A) through (F) of this paragraph, or participation as an accomplice of a person who commits, attempts, or conspires to commit such an offense; and

(2) except in extraordinary circumstances, do not include—

(A) an offense that consists of homicide, assault with intent to commit serious bodily injury, kidnapping, the taking of a hostage, or serious unlawful detention;

(B) an offense involving the use of a firearm (as such term is defined in section 921 of this title) if such use endangers a person other than the offender;

(C) an attempt or conspiracy to commit an offense described in subparagraphs (A) or (B) of this paragraph, or participation as an accomplice of a person who commits, attempts, or conspires to commit such an offense.

The court shall not take evidence with respect to, or otherwise consider, an issue under this subsection until the court determines the person is otherwise extraditable. Upon motion of the Attorney General or the person sought to be extradited, the United States district court may order the determination of any issue under this subsection by a judge of such court.

H.R. 3347, the Extradition Act of 1984, was approved by the House Committee on the Judiciary in June, 1984, but rejected by the House during closing sessions of the 98th Congress in 1984. It took a somewhat different approach from S. 1972. Section 3194 of H.R. 3347 provides:

(2) For the purposes of this section, a political offense does not include—

(A) a serious offense involving an attack against the life, physical integrity or liberty of internationally protected persons (as defined in section 1116 of this title), including diplomatic agents;

(B) an offense with respect to which a multilateral treaty obligates the United States to either extradite or submit for prosecution a person accused of the offense;

(C) an offense that consists of the manufacture, importation, distribution, or sale of narcotics or dangerous drugs;

(D) forceable sexual assault; or

(E) an offense that consists of intentional, direct participation in a wanton or indiscriminate act of violence with extreme indifference to the risk of causing death or serious bodily injury to persons not taking part in armed hostilities;

(F) an attempt or conspiracy to commit an offense described in subparagraphs (A) through (E) of this paragraph, or participation as an accomplice of a person who commits, attempts, or conspires to commit such an offense.

(3) The inclusion in paragraph (2) of this subsection of certain offenses does not preclude the exclusion of other offenses from the political offense category. In determining whether an offense is a political offense, the court shall consider, as of the time of the offense —

(A) the status (whether civilian, governmental, or military) of any victims of the alleged offense;

(B) the relationship of the alleged offender to a political organization;

(C) the existence of a civil uprising, rebellion, widespread civil unrest, or insurrection within the state requesting extradition;

(D) the motive of the alleged offender for the conduct alleged to constitute the offense;

(E) the nexus of such alleged conduct to the goals of a political organization; and

(F) the seriousness of the offense.

Both S. 1972 and H.R. 3347 employed what Professor Bassiouni has termed "the exception to the exception" in attempting to deal with the problem of the political offense exception and international terrorism. That is, they sought to identify those criminal acts that under no circumstances, or "except in extraordinary circumstances," would be considered political offenses. Noteworthy in this connection is section 3194(e)(2)(E) of H.R. 3347, which incorporated the concept found in the law of armed conflict that intentional, wanton, or reckless attacks against persons not taking part in armed hostilities are impermissible and cannot be characterized as political offenses. Both bills would have excluded from the political offense exception any offense covered by the counterterrorist conventions that obligate the United States either to extradite or to submit for prosecution a person accused of the offense.

S. 1972 went on to exclude, "except in extraordinary circumstances," crimes of violence. The term "extraordinary circumstances" is extremely vague, and it is unclear how the courts would apply it in practice. The legislative history of this provision indicates the drafters intended that this language, coupled with the burden on the accused to prove that his offense constituted a political offense by clear and convincing evidence, would have severely limited application of the doctrine. A report of the Senate Committee on Foreign Relations, which proposed this language, envisages that "extraordinary circumstances" would be limited to situations where the individual was forced to resort to the use of force because of a violation of his internationally recognized rights by the state requesting extradition.[91] This would be a drastic narrowing of the political offense exception and would, as a practical matter, likely limit application of the doctrine to situations where the requesting state has an egregious record in the human rights field. This limitation would adequately serve the humanitarian dimensions of the political offense exception, but would not necessarily be consistent with the principle that outside governments should remain neutral with respect to internal struggles for power.

Alternative approaches are available. For example, in the report of the International Law Association's Committee on International Terrorism, set forth and discussed above, sections 3, 4, and 5 would make it clear that no person would be permitted to escape trial or extradition on the ground of his political motivation, who, if he perfomed the same act as a soldier engaged in international armed conflict, or in a situation where the act would constitute a crime against humanity, would be subject to trial or extradition. If a provision along these lines were included in United States extradition treaties or in any legislation on extradition that may be forthcoming from Congress, a United States court would not be responsible for the anomaly that would result if it were to classify as a political offense an act that, under other circumstances, would be classified as a war crime or a crime against humanity.

Similarly, the International Criminal Law Committee of the American Bar Association's Section of International Law has advanced a proposal that would further incorporate into legislation on extradition considerations of the law of armed conflict as a limitation on application of the political offense doctrine.[92] In place of those acts now covered by the "extraordinary circumstances" language of S. 1972, the proposal would insert, in pertinent part, the following:

> (A) Except for acts committed in the course of a non-international armed conflict in furtherance of the objectives of the party to the conflict to which the person belongs and which do not violate the norms referred to in subparagraph (B) an offense that consists of homicide, assault with intent to commit serious bodily injury, kidnapping, serious unlawful detention, or an offense involving the use of firearms . . . if such use endangers a person other than the offender;
>
> (B)(i) an offense consisting of conduct which violates the provisions of subparagraph (1) of Article 3 Common to the Geneva Conventions of 12 August 1949 and any protocol additional thereto Relating to the Protection of Victims of Non-International Armed Conflict to which the United States is a party.

(ii) For purposes of this subparagraph, a non-international armed conflict within the meaning of Common Article 3 to the 1949 Geneva Conventions shall be an armed conflict which takes place within the territory of a foreign state between its armed forces and dissident armed forces or other armed groups which are under command responsible to a party to the conflict for the conduct of its subordinates. The term "armed conflict" does not apply to situations of internal disturbances and tensions, such as riots, isolated and sporadic acts of violence and other acts of a similar nature.

A virtue of these provisions is that they avoid excluding from the scope of the political offense doctrine virtually all acts of violence by combatants on the losing side of non-international armed conflicts, such as an insurrection, rebellion, or civil war—thus maintaining United States neutrality with respect to such conflicts. At the same time they preclude application of the doctrine to smaller scale outbreaks of violence and avoid any implication that police and military personnel are "fair game" in instances of violence not rising to the level of a non-international armed conflict.

For its part, H.R. 3347 went beyond the "exception to the exception" approach. Although it did not, strictly speaking, attempt to define a political offense, it did set forth a variety of criteria that courts would have been required to consider in determining whether an alleged criminal act was a political offense. The bill simply listed these criteria, however; it did not specify precisely how the courts are to apply them in their deliberations, nor what weight is to be given each of the criteria. The result is considerable confusion. For example, courts are to consider whether victims of an alleged offense are civilians, government officials, or military officials. Presumably, if they are civilians, the crime could not be classified as a political offense. On the other hand, if they are governmental or military officials, does this create a presumption in favor of a finding of a political offense? Similarly, the courts would be required to consider the motive of the alleged offender for the conduct alleged to constitute the offense. But to what end, and would consideration of the motive of the alleged offender be consistent with the general approach of United States criminal law jurisprudence which takes into account only the intent and not the motivation of an accused in determining guilt or innocence? The other criteria listed in H.R. 3347 raise similar difficulties of ambiguousness and lack of precision. They amount to an attempt to introduce rigid parameters to a doctrine that, courts around the world have discovered, demands flexible boundaries to reflect complex political and social variables. The attempt should be abandoned.

Whatever changes, if any, Congress may decide to make in the provisions of current legislation on international extradition, it appears highly likely that it will vest the decision-making authority on the political offense issue in courts rather than in the executive branch. However, as noted above, the United States is currently a party to several bilateral extradition treaties that expressly reserve such decision-making authority to the executive branch. The issue therefore arises whether these treaty provisions would continue in effect were new legislation on extradition to become law.

In their current form the bills introduced in Congress make no reference to these treaty provisions. Hence one could argue that the drafters of the legislation intended to invest the courts with decision-making authority over the political offense exception only in the absence of an express treaty provision reserving such authority to the executive branch. To the contrary, one might contend that these treaty provisions are simply incompatible with Congress' rejection of the executive branch's attempt to insert similar provisions in the legislation and that, under the so-called last-in-time rule,[93] the legislation, coming into force after the effective date of these treaties, must prevail.

This ambiguity should be eliminated from the legislation and not left to the courts to resolve. An express provision should be inserted declaring that decision-making authority on the political offense exception is reserved to the courts, despite any treaty provision to the contrary.

Finally, it should be noted that under existing law the term "treaty or convention for extradition" has been narrowly construed by the executive branch to apply only to treaties the primary purpose of which is to provide for extradition. Consequently, current United States policy permits extradition only on the basis of bilateral treaties. Apparently the reason for this provision is the United States' desire to retain the discretion to refuse extradition of persons to certain states that are parties to the counterterrorist conventions.[94] In declining to enter into bilateral extradition agreements with such states, the United States has effectuated this policy. As noted previously, however, none of the counterterrorist conventions contains an obligation to extradite. The decision whether to extradite is solely up to the requested state. It can choose, if it wishes, to refuse extradition and instead submit the accused to its law enforcement officials for purposes of prosecution.

Further, by declining to recognize the counterterrorist conventions as a possible basis for extradition, the United States unnecessarily hampers its own efforts to take the lead in combating terrorism. Most of these conventions require a request for extradition before the state party where an accused is found has any obligation to submit him to its appropriate authorities for purposes of prosecution. Accordingly, unless the United States is willing to make a request for extradition to a state party with which it does not have a bilateral extradition treaty, it can do nothing to induce such a state to prosecute the accused. The adverse impact on the effective functioning of the "extradite or prosecute" system established by these conventions could be considerable.

S. 1972 came directly to grips with this problem and made it clear that extradition clauses in the counterterrorist conventions would provide a basis for extradition under United States law. Such a provision should be part of any legislation eventually promulgated.

Efforts to deprive the courts entirely of the authority to decide what acts constitute a political offense or to circumscribe their authority by setting the boundaries of the political offense exception raise a larger and deeper issue: does the political offense exception to extradition serve any function that could not be performed by other doctrines of extradition law and practice? For example, it could be argued that the rights of an accused in situations involving armed rebellion against foreign governments can be protected by an inquiry as to whether the government is seeking his extradition for purposes of persecution for his political beliefs or by an examination of the foreign country's judicial system to determine whether it will afford the accused minimum standards of due process. These inquiries, the argument might continue, have always been the function of the secretary of state.[95] In the case of Great Britain, none of these problems exists, thus *McMullen, Mackin, Quinn,* and *Doherty* should have been extradited. By contrast, an Afghan who has shot a member of the Afghanistan army should not be extradited to Afghanistan because his trial would not be in accord with minimum standards of human rights.

If the sole purpose of the political offense exception were protection of the rights of an accused, this argument would have some persuasive effect. The secretary of state is in the best position to determine the motivation behind a particular request for extradition and is more aware whether conditions in the requesting country at the time of the extradition request comport with minimum standards of human rights. To be sure, the argument is still not necessarily conclusive, because one can contend that in a democratic society the judiciary is the proper institution to protect individuals from the political vagaries of governments. We shall return to this issue later in the study.

But the rights of an accused are not the only nor necessarily the most important consideration underlying the political offense exception. Another, as we have previously seen, is the principle that outside governments should remain neutral with respect to internal struggles for power. In other words, a principled application of the political offense exception might require the United States to refuse to extradite an individual accused of armed rebellion despite its desire to promote cooperative relations with the requesting country.

Ironically, such a stance may be required in the interest of an effective antiterrorist policy. As noted above, the effort to exclude the courts from deciding whether an accused has committed a political offense was precipitated by State Department displeasure with the *McMullen* and *Mackin* decisions. In testimony before the Senate and the House, the executive branch contended that these decisions seriously undermined United States' efforts to combat terrorism. But, in debates in international forums, the United States has not claimed that armed attacks against *military* targets constitute terrorism. To the contrary, the draft convention against terrorism that the United States introducd in the United Nations General Assembly after the murder of the Israeli Olympic competitors at Munich in 1972 would have expressly excluded any attack by or against armed forces from the scope of its coverage.[96] This was done in part to meet the concerns of Third World countries that the United States initiative was aimed at suppressing "wars of national liberation" in southern Africa and the Middle East. In draft legislation Congress also has expressly excluded from its definition of "international terrorism" an act "committed in the course of military or paramilitary operations directed essentially against military forces or military targets of a state or an organized armed group."[97]

This is not to say that the United States should support IRA attacks against the British military. It is to suggest the United States may wish to hesitate before becoming involved, through the extradition process, in the internal struggle for power in Northern Ireland or other areas of the world. Such involvement might lend a measure of support to those who claim that the United States' antiterrorist effort is directed primarily toward suppressing liberation movements around the world. The actual focus of United States' concern has been more narrow.

By contrast, Abu Eain's setting off a bomb in a marketplace in Tiberius clearly qualified as a terrorist act under any definition. Although committed on behalf of the Palestine Liberation Organization, under the name of liberating "Greater Palestine," it targeted innocent civilians rather than military personnel or property. This was predominantly a common crime, and the courts were correct in excluding it from the political offense exception.

Similarly, the acts of Mr. Quinn in sending letter bombs and placing bombs in public places so that they would endanger the lives and physical well-being of civilians should not have been classified as political offenses. Any legislation on extradition forthcoming from Congress should support this proposition in no uncertain terms.

OTHER SELECTED COUNTRIES

United Kingdom

In March, 1979, the home secretary of the United Kingdom announced the appointment of an independent working group to review the laws and practices of extradition in Great Britain with a view to possible reform.[98] The working group held eighteen meetings and issued a report in May of 1982.

The working group's report contains a number of observations and recommendations relative not only to the United Kingdom but also to the United States and other countries. Although the study was not undertaken with specific reference to extradition and international terrorism, much of it has special significance for this area, and it is on these aspects of the report that we will focus our attention.

British law and practice includes a variety of extradition arrangements. There is, not surprisingly, an extensive network of bilateral extradition treaties.[99] With respect to some countries—for example, the United States—a bilateral agreement is required. As to the Commonwealth countries, however, the United Kingdom is "able to operate satisfactory extradition arrangements . . . on the basis of substantially uniform legislation unsupported by any kind of formal agreement."[100] Although there have been proposals for a Commonwealth treaty on extradition, the view has prevailed that, since Commonwealth countries have so much in common in their traditions of law and standards of justice, extradition arrangements can and should be based on reciprocity and uniform legislation; under this view it would be superfluous to supplant such arrangements by treaty.[101]

Although the United Kingdom has not become a party to the European Convention on Extradition, it has ratified the Hague and Montreal Conventions on Civil Aviation, as well as the United Nations Convention for the Prevention and Punishment of Crimes Against Internationally Protected Persons, Including Diplomatic Agents. At this writing the United Kingdom has signed but not yet ratified the Hostages Convention and the Convention for the Physical Protection of Nuclear Materials. As previously noted, all of these conventions can be used for the purpose of extradition.

The United Kingdom has special arrangements with the Republic of Ireland, based on reciprocal legislation, for the return of offenders.[102] These arrangements provide for the return of persons accused or convicted of indictable offenses, or of offenses punishable on summary conviction with six months imprisonment, for which there is a corresponding offense under the law of the requested country. Although these arrangements contain a safeguard against the return of political offenders, other procedural requirements common to extradition, such as the need to establish a prima-facie case against an accused person, are omitted. According to the working group's report, this "simple and expeditious procedure is justified by the special circumstances of the two countries, in particular the similarity of their systems of law, their geographic proximity and the ease of communication and lack of immigration control."[103]

Also noteworthy is British legislation, which confers on the courts in Northern Ireland jurisdiction over certain offenses committed in the Irish Republic and which also gives courts in Great Britain as well as in Northern Ireland jurisdiction in certain circumstances where a British citizen causes an explosion in the republic or when such a citizen conspires to cause an explosion in the republic.[104] The Republic of Ireland's criminal law contains parallel provisions for jurisdiction over such offenses committed in Northern Ireland.

Of particular interest is the report's discussion of so-called ad hoc extradition—that is, extradition based on the requested state's municipal law to a state with which no extradition agreement is in force.[105] The report points out that many foreign states—including at the least the Republic of Ireland, Japan, Finland, Norway, Denmark, and Sweden—are able to extradite both on the basis of treaties and, where no treaty exists, on the basis of their municipal law. The report lists the following factors in favor of this approach:

a. It is in the interests of all nations to bring offenders to trial, and to this extent the wider the options the better;

b. The negotiation of complex treaties, which is time-consuming and expensive in terms of manpower and other resources, could be avoided in respect of countries with which the United Kingdom has little or no regular extradition traffic;

c. *ad hoc* arrangements offer greater flexibility in taking account of changes in other countries' standards of justice;

d. *ad hoc* arrangements would provide cover while treaties were negotiated, or re-negotiated.[106]

The report also points out that the existence of a power to surrender in the absence of a treaty would reduce British reluctance to make an extradition request to a country with which it had no treaty, since such countries may request that reciprocal facilities should in principle be provided. It further suggests that, as a result of adoption of ad hoc arrangements, "there would be fewer countries to which criminals could escape in the certain knowledge that recovery was not possible under extradition procedures."[107]

The report recognizes that British statutory safeguards for the fugitive, such as exclusion of the political offense, would have to apply to ad hoc arrangements just as they do to extradition under treaty arrangements. The more difficult question it identifies is "how to decide whether in principle extradition to a requesting State should be contemplated, having regard to its standards of administration of justice, its prison conditions and its willingness to reciprocate."[108] The report suggests that any legislation on ad hoc extradition should require that the secretary of state be satisfied, before issuing an order to proceed and before surrendering a fugitive, that the standards of justice and penal administration in the requesting state are such that it would be in the interest of justice to surrender the fugitive. The report rejects, however, any statutory requirements of reciprocity, on the ground that the United Kingdom might wish to extradite notwithstanding the inability of the requesting state to reciprocate because its law allows it to extradite only pursuant to a treaty.

The report recommends the introduction, in the interest of flexibility, of a system of ad hoc extradition into British law with respect to those states with which the likely amount of extradition traffic would not justify negotiating an extradition treaty. The ad hoc system also has the advantage, according to the report, that it would enable the United Kingdom to consider a request for extradition from a state with which a treaty was in the process of being negotiated or re-negotiated. The report concedes that embarrassment could arise "if a request which was on the face of it entirely straightforward had to be blocked at the outset because it came from a country with unacceptable standards of justice."[109] In practice, however, the report suggests, a foreign state would take "preliminary soundings" about the possibility of obtaining extradition under ad hoc arrangements and would rarely press the case to the stage of formal rejection.

The report envisages that ad hoc arrangements would work as follows:

> On receipt of an approach from the State concerned, a decision would be taken (on the basis of the information available to the Government, supplemented as necessary by enquiry of the United Kingdom representative in that State) as to whether the State was one from which the United Kingdom Government would be prepared to entertain an application. At the same time, a view would be taken on whether the offense appeared to be extraditable in United Kingdom law, whether there had been sufficient preliminary judicial scrutiny in the requesting State (i.e. whether an acceptable warrant of arrest existed there), and whether there was any other obvious bar to extradition. If the United Kingdom was satisfied on these points authority could be given for provisional arrest. There would need to be a time limit at the end of which the magistrate would be required to discharge the fugitive if a formal request, and the supporting documents, had not by then been received . . . Meanwhile a diplomatic approach would be made drawing the requesting State's attention to our requirements as to evidence, etc., and seeking assurances with regard to the statutory safeguards. We think that this need not be a time consuming procedure — the time limit on provisional arrest would no doubt serve as an incentive to speedy exchanges.[110]

As to the political offense exception, the report recommends that any new extradition law should contain a safeguard against surrender for political offenses, but no attempt should be made to define the term "political offense" in the statute. The courts would make the decision whether a particular offense was of a political character. However, should the courts decide to commit the fugitive for surrender, the secretary of state should still have the authority to decide not to extradite the accused.[111]

The report declined to recommend a provision that the murder or attempted murder of a head of state should not be considered a political offense. According to the report, circumstances could vary, and each case should be determined on its merits by the courts and the secretary of state.[112]

Austria

The new Austrian law on extradition has been briefly considered previously in the discussion of the political offense exception. In this section we examine some other provisions of the Austrian law relevant to extradition and international terrorism.

The Austrian Law on Extradition and Mutual Assistance in Criminal Matters (hereafter ARHG) became effective on July 1, 1980.[113] It represents the first comprehensive statutory treatment of these matters for Austria and contains a number of innovative provisions.

Under the ARHG treaties take priority. That is, concerning requests for assistance that are based on a treaty obligation, the ARHG applies only to the extent that it is consistent with specific treaty provisions.

At the administrative level, the Ministry of Justice has a primary responsibility for implementing the ARHG. In contrast with the practice followed in some Anglo-American systems, the involvement of the Austrian Ministry of Foreign Affairs is of lesser importance. Its role is largely limited to the forwarding of communications through diplomatic channels when custom or treaty establishes this manner of communication. However, diplomatic channels are usually avoided with respect to West European countries because communications with them are often carried out between the ministries of justice, or directly between the cooperating agencies and courts.

Austria grants extradition by reciprocity to a larger number of countries than those with whom it is bound by treaty. But in practice most extradition and mutual assistance activity occurs between Austria and states with whom Austria is bound by treaties.

Austria is a party to only a few bilateral extradition treaties. Its three separate treaties with the common law countries of Australia, Canada, and Great Britain require, in keeping with the legal systems of these countries, prima-facie evidence of guilt for extradition; they also enumerate extraditable offenses. For its part, Austria retains the right under these treaties to refuse extradition of its nationals and in cases involving possible use of the death penalty. The older treaty with the United States contains no explicit exception regarding the death penalty,[114] but in practice Austria would demand a guarantee from the United States that no death penalty would be imposed.

Recent extradition treaties between Austria and Poland and Hungary represent "something of a pioneering effort" in that they grant Austria the right to refuse extradition when this action would violate other international agreements.[115] The purpose of this provision is to ensure compliance with the Refugees Convention and the European Human Rights Convention.

A major limitation on extradition is the ARHG's requirement of reciprocity. Under case law predating ARHG, interpreting reciprocity as a general principle of international law, reciprocity worked both ways, since it not only was a condition for the granting of assistance, particularly extradition, but it also made it illegal for Austrian authorities to request extradition in the absence of reciprocity. The ARHG has revised the latter interpretation and permits Austrian authorities to request cooperation in the absence of reciprocity when such cooperation is urgently needed. These requests must inform the requested state of Austria's inability to reciprocate, since the ARHG provides no exceptions from reciprocity regarding foreign requests. In determining whether reciprocity is guaranteed in a particular case, the Austrian courts examine applicable international agreements, the domestic law of the requesting state, individual guarantees given by the requesting state, and actual practice.

It must be remembered that Austrian criminal jurisdiction is far-reaching. Therefore, in the event Austria decides not to honor a request for extradition, it may itself subject the accused to criminal prosecution. For example, the criminal code subjects all Austrian citizens to possible criminal liability for offenses committed abroad.[116] The criminal code also utilizes the protective principle of international criminal jurisdiction to guard against offenses that, although committed abroad, might endanger the political and economic foundations of Austria.[117] Further, under the universality principle, Austria assumes residuary and even primary jurisdiction over certain offenses regardless of their place of commission or the status of the offender.[118]

With respect to the universality principle, section 64 of the Austrian criminal code enumerates all extraterritorial offenses over which Austria is bound to exercise jurisdiction on the basis of existing international agreements. For future agreements in the international criminal law area, section 64 contains a general clause that such offenses come under Austrian jurisdiction.

Under section 65 of the criminal code, Austria exercises residuary jurisdiction over extraterritorial offenses that are punishable both according to Austrian law and according to the law of the place of commission, if the offender was an Austrian citizen at the time of commission or at the time of initiation of the Austrian proceedings. It also may exercise residuary jurisdiction if a non-Austrian offender is apprehended in Austria and his extradition cannot be effected even though the offense is extraditable. Since residuary jurisdiction under section 65 is available only for extraditable offenses, it excludes political, fiscal, and military offenses. Typically, such jurisdiction is exercised when Austria offers extradition but the foreign state declines to request it.

Under section 9, paragraph 3, of the ARHG, prosecution based only on section 65 is discretionary, as long as "public interests do not oppose the refrainment from prosecution, in particular, punishment is not indicated to deter the commission of offenses by others." This is because it may be difficult to obtain sufficient evidence from the place of commission of the alleged act to convict the accused.

Another innovative feature of the ARHG is that the availability of Austrian criminal jurisdiction, although constituting an important ground of refusal, no longer creates an absolute bar to extradition. More far reaching is section 13 of the ARHG, which prohibits the use of deportation as the means of circumventing extradition. This prohibition applies not only when a formal request has been made by another state, but also when "sufficient reasons for the initiation of such a proceeding are given." Such protection against deportation in lieu of extradition was viewed by the drafters of the ARHG as part of the due process protection accorded fugitives.[119] At the same time the ARHG creates the possibility of voluntary extradition, thus eliminating the need for a formal proceeding, subject to a court's determination that the accused's consent is truly voluntary.

As noted above, under the ARHG, extradition is generally disallowed when Austria has jurisdiction over the offense, whether or not prosecution has been initiated. This rule is subject, however, to an important exception. Austrian jurisdiction is not a bar to extradition when a trial in the requesting state would be more expedient or if a penalty could be imposed more fairly in a trial there. A prime example is a case where there is a concurrence of several offenses, some of which are not subject to Austrian jurisdiction. The rehabilitation of the offender is the motivating factor for this exception. It also serves as a primary basis for the rule against extradition of nationals.[120]

Section 22 of the ARHG exempts fugitives from extradition for humanitarian reasons. This provision covers situations where extradition "would constitute an undue hardship for him, on account of his youthful age . . . his domestic domicile of long standing, or for other serious reasons arising from his personal circumstance."

Under section 19 of the ARHG, extradition is barred if there is reason to believe that:

> 1. The criminal proceeding in the requesting state would not comply or has not complied with the principles of articles 3 [prohibiting torture or inhuman or degrading treatment or punishment] and 6 [setting forth a variety of due process protections] of the Convention for the Protection of Human Rights and Fundamental Freedoms . . .

2. The penalty or preventive measure imposed or to be expected in the requesting state would be enforced in a manner not in compliance with the requirements of article 3 of the Convention for the Protection of Human Rights and Fundamental Freedoms . . .

3. The person to be extradited would be exposed in the requesting state to persecution on account of his descent, race, religion, association with a particular ethnic or social group, his nationality, or on account of his political views, or would have to expect other serious disadvantages from any one of these reasons . . .

Section 20 of the ARHG prohibits extradition unless non-imposition of the death penalty is guaranteed by the requesting state. The same bar applies as well to penalties or preventive measures that could violate article 3 of the European Human Rights Convention.

Notes

1. A challenge to this conclusion has recently been raised in a draft report of the International Law Association's Committee on International Terrorism, as we shall see later in this study.
2. See Lillich and Paxman, "State Responsibility for Injuries to Aliens Occasioned by Terrorist Activities," *American University Law Review* 26 (1977):217, 297–305.
3. H.M.S.O. London, Cmd. 3008.
4. For a discussion of the Commonwealth Scheme, see Shearer, "The Current Framework of International Extradition: A Brief Study of Regional Arrangements and Multilateral Treaties," in M. C. Bassiouni and V. Nanda, *A Treatise on International Criminal Law,* vol. 1 (1973), pp. 326, 328–30.
5. For a discussion of the Nordic States' Scheme, see id., at 332–33.
6. Id., at 332.
7. See Shearer, supra note 4.
8. Council of Europe, Eur. T.S. No. 24.
9. This information is derived from the report "A Review of the Law and Practice of Extradition in the United Kingdom," prepared by a working group appointed by the British home secretary in March 1979 and kindly supplied this writer by Michael Abbell, then Associate Director, Office of International Affairs, Criminal Division, Department of Justice. The report of the working group was submitted to the home secretary in May 1982. The information regarding parties to the European Convention on Extradition is to be found at page 83.
10. Id.
11. Id.
12. See Shearer, supra note 4, at 331–32.
13. Art. 33 of the Inter-American Convention on Extradition.
14. The text of the convention is reprinted in 20 I.L.M. 723 (1981).
15. Art. 1.
16. Art. 2(1).
17. Art. 2(2).
18. Art. 3(1).
19. Art. 13(1).
20. Art. 13(1)(c).
21. Art. 4(4).
22. Art. 6.
23. See, generally, Barbero-Santos, "*General Introduction and Definition of 'Asylum'* " in M. C. Bassiouni and V. Nanda, *A Treatise on International Criminal Law,* vol. 2, (1973), p. 335.

24. U.N. Doc. A/PV 2202, at 135-36 (1973).
25. See Evans, "Perspectives on International Terrorism," *Willamette Law Review* 17, (1980): 151, 161.
26. For an approach along these lines, see Lockwood, "The Model American Convention on the Prevention and Punishment of Certain Serious Forms of Violence Jeopardizing Fundamental Rights and Freedoms, *Rutgers Law Journal* 13, (1982): 579.
27. Treaty of Extradition, Mar. 1, 1933, United States-Albania, 49 Stat. 3313; T.S. No. 902; LNTS 195, entered into force Nov. 14, 1935. For a table of U.S. treaties of extradition, see 18 U.S.C. §3181.
28. See 18 U.S.C. §3181 and Factor v. Laubenheimer, 290 U.S. 276, 287 (1933).
29. On June 28, 1984, the Senate agreed to a resolution advising and consenting to ratification of the Treaty. See *International Law Perspective* 2 (June, 1984). According to information supplied this writer by the Office of Treaty Affairs, Department of State, the president ratified the treaty on August 17, 1984.
30. See article III of Treaty on Extradition Between the United States of America and Japan, March 3, 1978, 31 U.S.T. 392; T.I.A.S. No. 9625, entered into force Mar. 26, 1980.
31. Re double criminality, see M. C. *Bassiouni, International Extradition: United States Law and Practice,* vol. 7, (1983): §3-1-3-6.
32. See art. VI(1) of Treaty on Extradition Between the United States and Japan, supra note 30.
33. Art. IV(1)(1), *id.*
34. L. Oppenheim, *International Law,* vol. 1, 8th ed., 707-8, (Lauterpacht, 1955).
35. C. Van den Wijngaert, *The Political Offense Exception to Extradition* 2 (1980).
36. Id., at 3.
37. Id., at 4.
38. Id., at 5.
39. As quoted in id., at 7.
40. Id.
41. Id., at 12.
42. Id.
43. Id., at 14.
44. Id., at 111-32.
45. Id., at 111.
46. 1 Q.B. 149, 5 British Law Cases, International Law Cases 556.
47. 2 Q.B. 415, 5 British Law Cases, International Law Cases 572.
48. Queen's Bench, 21 International Law Reports 240 (1954).
49. Regina v. Governor of Brixton Prison, ex parte Schtraks, Queen's Bench, 33 International Law Reports 319 (1967); Schtraks v. The Government of Israel, House of Lords, 33 International Law Reports 332 (1967).
50. As quoted in the report, "A review of the Law and Practice of Extradition in the United Kingdom," supra note 9 at 34.
51. Id.
52. Regina v. Governor of Pentonville Prison, ex parte Tzu-Tsai Cheng, Queen's Bench, 1 All. English Reports 935 (1973) and Tzu-Tsai Cheng v. Governor of Pentonville Prison, House of Lords, 2 All. English Reports 204 (1973).
53. C. Van den Wijngaert, supra note 35, at 115-16.
54. Id., at 116.
55. 311 F. 2d 547 (5th Cir. 1962), cert. denied, 373 U.S. 914 (1963).
56. 311 F. 2d at 560.
57. 217 F. Supp. 717 (S.D.N.Y. 1963).
58. C. Van den Wijngaert, supra note 35, at 117-18.
59. Artukovic v. Boyle, 107 F. Supp. 11 (S.D. Cal. 1952), rev'd sub nom. Ivancevic v. Artukovic, 211 F. 2d 565 (9th Cir. 1954), on remand sub nom. Artukovic v. Boyle, 140 F. Supp. 245 (S.D. Cal. 1956), aff'd sub nom. Karadzole v. Artukovic, 247 F. 2d 198 (9th Cir. 1957), rev'd, 355 U.S. 898 (1958), on remand sub nom. United States v. Artukovic, 170 F. Supp. 383 (S.D. Cal. 1959).
60. In re McMullen, Mag. No. 3-78-1099 MG (N.D.Cal. May 11, 1979) (unreported).
61. Id., at 4.

62. Mag. No. 79 M 175, Dec. 18, 1979, reprinted in Abu Eain v. Adams, 529 F Supp. 685, 688 (N.D. Ill. 1980).
63. Id., at 21, 529 F. Supp. at 695.
64. Abu Eain v. Adams, 529 F. Supp. 685 (N.D. Ill. 1980).
65. Mag. No. 80 Cr. Misc. 1, Aug. 13, 1981 (unreported).
66. Mackin v. Grant, 668 F. 2d 122 (2d Cir. 1981).
67. Quinn v. Robinson, No. C-82-6688 RPA, Oct. 3, 1983 (unreported). At this writing the case is on appeal to the Ninth Circuit.
68. *Matter of Doherty By Gov. of United Kingdom,* 599 F. Supp. 270 (D.C.N.Y. 1984).
69. Id., at 276.
70. Id.
71. Id.
72. Id., at 275-76.
73. C. Van den Wijngaert, supra note 35, at 120.
74. Judgment of Apr. 14, 1975, Cour d'appel, Paris (unpublished). See E. McDowell, *Digest of United States Practice in International Law* (1975), p. 168, for a discussion of the facts and holding.
75. Judgment of Nov. 16, 1977, Cour d'appel, Paris (unpublished), reprinted in appendix, *1983 Michigan Yearbook of International Legal Studies, Transnational Aspects of Criminal Procedure,* at 349.
76. Judgment of Oct. 11, 1971, No. 1343-79, Cour d'appel, Cass. acc. 1 re. The text of the opinion is reprinted in the appendix referred to supra note 75, at 376. The quote is from page 379.
77. Carbonneau, "The Political Offense Exception as Applied in French Cases Dealing with the Extradition of Terrorists," *1983 Michigan Yearbook of International Studies,* supra note 75, at 209, 233.
78. C. Van den Wijngaert, supra note 25, at 125.
79. Id., at 126.
80. As quoted in id., at 126.
81. For an extensive discussion of the Austrian Act and other aspects of Austrian extradition law and practice, see E. Palmer, *The Austrian Law on Extradition and Mutual Assistance in Criminal Matters* (1983).
82. Id., at 90.
83. Id., at 90-91.
84. Id., at 59, fn 169.
85. C. Van den Wijngaert, supra note 35, at 132.
86. The report of the committee will be published by the International Law Association as part of the proceedings of its 1984 meeting in Paris. Also, before that time, with the kind permission of the ILA, the report will appear as part of a symposium on legal aspects of international terrorism in *Terrorism — An International Journal* 7, No. 2: 199.
87. E.g., Extradition Treaty, May 4, 1978, United States-Mexico, art. X, §1, 31 U.S.T. 5059, T.I.A.S. No. 9656, Entered into force Jan. 25, 1980.
88. S. 1639, 97th Cong., 1st sess., *Congressional Record* 127 (1981): 9960-62.
89. See, generally, *Extradition Act of 1981: Hearings on S. 1639 Before the Senate Comm. on the Judiciary,* 97th Cong., 1st sess, (1981).
90. See id., at 89, 90 (Letter from the American Civil Liberties Union)
91. S. Rep. No. 97-475, 97th Cong., 2d sess. 8 (1982).
92. A copy of the report of the International Criminal Law Committee was kindly supplied this writer by Waldemor A. Solf, chairman of the committee.
93. Under Article VI of the Constitution, both laws and treaties are to be the "supreme Law of the Land." This has been interpreted to mean that federal laws and treaties are of equal force and that therefore the maxim *lex posterior derogat priori* applies. That is, a later inconsistent statute will be given effect over a prior treaty obligation. See Moser v. United States, 341 U.S. 41, 45 (1951); Clark v. Allen, 331 U.S. 513, 508-9 (1947); The Head Money Cases, 112 U.S. 580, 597 (1884).
94. See Bassiouni, "Remarks to the Panel on International Procedures for the Apprehension and Rendition of Fugitive Offenders," *Proceedings of the American Society of International Law* (1980): 274, 277.

95. See, e.g., hearings on S. 1639, supra note 84, at 29, 36–63 (statement of William M. Hannay).

96. *Draft Convention for the Prevention and Punishment of Certain Acts of International Terrorism (Draft Convention to Prevent the Spread of Terrorist Violence)*, U.N. Doc. A/C. 6 L. 850 (1972).

97. S. 333, 96th Cong., 1st sess. §5 (1979).

98. See report, "A Review of the Law and Practice of Extradition in the United Kingdom," supra note 9.

99. According to the report, the United Kingdom had, as of May 1982, bilateral extradition agreements with 43 other countries. There was, however, only about a dozen countries with which there was any significant amount of extradition traffic. Id. at 5.

100. Id., at 4.
101. Id.
102. Id., at 2–3.
103. Id., at 2.
104. Id., at 3.
105. Id., at 6–8.
106. Id., at 7.
107. Id.
108. Id.
109. Id., at 8.
110. Id.
111. Id., at 40.
112. Id.

113. See E. Palmer, supra note 81, at 1. The discussion of the Austrian law which follows is taken largely from Palmer's study.

114. See Treaty for the Extradition of Fugitives from Justice, and Exchange of Notes Concerning the Death Penalty, Jan. 31, 1930, United States-Austria, 46 Stat. 2779; T.S. No. 822; 5 Bevans 358; 106 League of Nations Treaty Series 379. Entered into force Sept. 11, 1930. Supplementary Extradition Convention, May 19, 1934, United States–Austria, 49 Stat. 2710; T.S. No. 873; 5 Bevans 378; 153 LNTS 247. Entered into force Sept. 5, 1934.

115. E. Palmer, supra note 81, at 16.
116. Id., at 26.
117. Id., at 26–27.
118. Id., at 27.
119. Id., at 32.
120. Id., at 47.

CHAPTER 3

Methods of Rendition Other Than Extradition

As indicated earlier, and as we shall see in greater detail later in this study, extradition has not been the most favored method of rendition of international terrorists. In this chapter we explore some of the legal dimensions of exclusion and deportation, the most popular alternatives to extradition. Illegal methods of rendition — that is, abduction and unlawful seizure — have apparently not yet been utilized with respect to international terrorists. Nonetheless, to the extent that extradition, exclusion, and deportation fail to bring international terrorists to justice, the temptation for states to resort to illegal methods of rendition will be considerable. Accordingly, we briefly examine these methods at the end of this chapter.

Exclusion and Deportation

The late Alona Evans characterized extradition based upon treaties or extradition statutes establishing procedures for the purpose of rendition per se as a "formal" method of rendition.[1] Professor Evans noted further that

> The extradition process is characterized and, indeed, limited by adherence to a number of established principles which constitute the customary international law on the subject. For example, there are the principles of double criminality, evidence of criminality, specialty, political defense, double jeopardy, time limit on detention, nonsurrender of nationals, and pending process against the accused in the requested State.[2]

By contrast, Professor Evans characterized exclusion and deportation as "quasi-formal" methods of rendition.[3] Although they involve established procedures, these are not designed for the purpose of cooperation in furthering the international criminal justice system. Rather, both exclusion and deportation are civil processes, designed for immigration control and dominated by the executive. As a consequence, exclusion and deportation proceedings utilized for rendition purposes do not apply criminal justice standards, either with respect to the interests of the states involved or to protection of the accused.

Unlike extradition, exclusion and deportation rarely involve a formal request by a state seeking return of an alleged offender. On the contrary, exclusion and deportation are effected at the instance of a territorial state. Nonetheless, in many instances, this informal rendition may be carried out in response to a request from a state seeking the return of an accused. Such a request may take the form merely of an expression of interest by law enforcement officials.

This widespread use of exclusion and deportation as a method of rendition raises a number of issues under international and national law. We turn first to the international area.

INTERNATIONAL LAW

The primary, but by no means the only, treaties relevant to the use of exclusion and deportation as an alternative to extradition are the Convention Relating to the Status of Refugees[4] and the Protocol Relating to the Status of Refugees.[5] The protocol revises the convention so as to make it applicable to events occurring after January 1, 1951.[6] Under article 1 of the convention, a refugee is defined as a person who

> "owing to a well-founded fear of being persecuted for reasons of race, religion, nationality, membership of a particular racial group or political opinion, is outside the country of his nationality and is unable or, owing to such fear, is unwilling to avail himself of the protection of that country; or who, not having a nationality and being outside the country of his former habitual residence or as a result of such events, is unable or, owing to such fear, is unwilling to return to it."

A threshold question, then, in exclusion and deportation cases is whether the person sought to be excluded or deported qualifies as a "refugee."

If a person qualifies as a refugee but is unlawfully in the country of refuge and thus subject to deportation, articles 31–33 of the convention impose limitations on the refuge state's authority to expel him:

Article 31

> 1. The Contracting States shall not impose penalties, on account of their illegal entry or presence, on refugees who, coming directly from a territory where their life or freedoom was threatened in the sense of article 1, enter

or are present in their territory without authorization, provided they present themselves without delay to the authorities and show good cause for their illegal entry or presence.

2. The Contracting States shall not apply to the movement of such refugees restrictions other than those which are necessary and such restrictions shall only be applied until their status in the country is regularized or they obtain admission into another country. The Contracting States shall allow such refugees a reasonable period and all the necessary facilities to obtain admission into another country.

Article 32

1. The Contracting States shall not expel a refugee lawfully in their territory save on grounds of national security or public order.

2. The expulsion of such a refugee shall be only in pursuance of a decision reached in accordance with due process of law. Except where compelling reasons of national security otherwise require, the refugee shall be allowed to submit evidence to clear himself, and to appeal to and be represented for the purpose before competent authority or a person or persons specially designated by the competent authority.

3. The Contracting States shall allow such a refugee a reasonable period within which to seek legal admission into another country. The Contracting States reserve the right to apply during that period such internal measures as they may deem necessary.

Article 33

1. No Contracting States shall expel or return ("refouler") a refugee in any manner whatsoever to the frontiers of territories where his life or freedom would be threatened on account of his race, religion, nationality, membership of a particular social group or political opinion.

2. The benefit of the present provision may not, however, be claimed by a refugee whom there are reasonable grounds for regarding as a danger to the security of the country in which he is, or who, having been convicted by a final judgment of a particularly serious crime, constitutes a danger to the community of that country.

Accordingly, in exclusion and deportation cases where the state of refuge is a party to the convention and protocol, an accused who can show that he is a refugee may be able to bar his rendition if he can prove that there is a likelihood that he might be persecuted in the state of destination. As we shall see below, the United States Refugee Act of 1980 has incorporated this defense into national law.

Professor Bassiouni has suggested that the use of exclusion and deportation as alternatives to extradition may, under certain circumstances, violate international human rights law.[7] He notes, for example, the following provisions of the Universal Declaration of Human Rights:

Article 3

Everyone has the right to life, liberty, and the security of person.

Article 9

No one shall be subject to arbitrary arrest, detention or exile.

Article 12

No one shall be subject to arbitrary interference with his privacy, family, home or correspondence, nor to a tax upon his honor and reputation. Everyone has the right to the protection of the law against such interference or attacks.

In Professor Bassiouni's view, these provisions protect the individual from arbitrary action of the host state regardless of the individual's legal status in the host country. Exclusion and deportation, unless carried out in accordance with procedures designed to protect the rights of an accused, may constitute arbitrary action.

Similarly, Colin Warbrick has recently pointed to provisions in the European Convention on Human Rights that arguably contain protection against exclusion and deportation as an alternative to extradition or what he terms "irregular extradition."[8] He notes the argument that irregular return of a fugitive is not "lawful" under article 5 of the convention. In pertinent part article 5 provides:

Everyone has the right to liberty and security of person. No one shall be deprived of his liberty save in the following cases and in accordance with the procedure prescribed by law:

(a) The lawful detention of a person after conviction by a competent court . . .

(c) The lawful arrest or detention of a person effected for the purpose of bringing him before the competent legal authority . . .

Warbrick notes further Dr. Paul O'Higgins' contention that a seizure of a person abroad might not be "in accordance with a procedure prescribed by law" and that a "competent court" cannot be determined solely by reference to the municipal law of a state but must mean "competent in the light of international law."[9] For his part, however, Warbrick rejects these contentions. Among other things he notes that the European Commission on Human Rights has not interpreted the convention along the lines suggested by Dr. O'Higgins. Rather the European Commission's review of "lawfulness" has been limited to reviewing whether the authorizing rule of the national system was truly a "law."[10]

NATIONAL LAW

As noted in the previous section, although exclusion and deportation may be subject to international law norms contained in the Convention and Protocol Relating to the Status of Refugees and other applicable legal instruments, these methods of rendition are primarily domestic in nature and hence governed by national law. In this section, therefore, we turn to United States law on exclusion and deportation as well as to the law of selected foreign countries.

United States

Before discussing United States law and practice, it should be noted that, as we shall see in greater detail in Part II of this study, the United States has not been in the forefront of those countries that have utilized exclusion and deportation as alternatives to extradition.[11] Nonetheless, these methods have been used by United States officials and in circumstances that have raised serious legal questions.

At first blush, the distinction between exclusion and deportation seems simple enough. Exclusion applies to persons who are seeking to enter the United States, while deportation applies to persons already in the United States. In practice, however, it may be difficult to determine whether a person is already "in" the United States if he has crossed the border but not yet reported to an inspection station. A prime example would be the Haitians who have arrived in the United States in small boats and sought refugee status.[12] The distinction may be significant because deportation hearings afford more protection to an alien than an exclusion proceeding does. For example, in deportation hearings, the government bears the burden of proving the alien is deportable; by contrast, in exclusion proceedings, except for returning resident aliens, the alien bears the burden of establishing admissibility, and the Supreme Court has held that aliens seeking admissibility are not covered by the Fifth Amendment's due process clause because they are not in the United States.[13]

One drawback to the use of exclusion as a method of rendition is that the alien can be returned only to the country from which he came.[14] Accordingly, if the alien has committed a crime in a country other than his country of origin, and that country seeks his return for prosecution, exclusion will not be available as an alternative to extradition.

It is more difficult under United States law to use deportation as an alternative to extradition. As previously noted, the Supreme Court has held that the due process clause of the Fifth Amendment applies to deportation hearings. Moreover, the statutory law of the United States provides that the government must establish deportability of an alien by clear and convincing evidence and that the decision of an immigration judge must be based on reasonable, substantive, and probative evidence.[15] Further, even if found deportable, the alien is allowed to designate a country to which he wishes to be deported. Accordingly, if the designated country accepts him, and it is not the state seeking his return for an alleged offense, an attempted use of deportation as an alternative to extradition will be unsuccessful. Lastly, as in the case of exclusion, an alien cannot be deported to a country where he will be subject to persecution and he may apply for asylum.[16]

Some of the difficulties in using deportation as an alternative to extradition are demonstrated by the case of *McMullen*. After the Magistrate determined that McMullen could not be extradited to the United Kingdom because his acts fell within the political offense exception, the United States Government attempted to deport him to the Republic of Ireland. An immigration judge granted McMullen's application for withholding of deportation, but the Board of Immigration Appeals reversed. On appeal, the Ninth Circuit granted McMullen's petition for withholding of deportation, holding (a) factual findings under the Refugee Act of 1980 are subject to review under the substantial evidence rule; and (b) substantial evidence did not support the board's finding that McMullen had failed to show a sufficient likelihood of persecution for his political beliefs if he were deported to the Republic of Ireland. In his petition McMullen alleged that the Provisional Wing of the Irish Republic Army (PIRA) would regard him as a traitor for dropping his membership, that the PIRA systematically tortured and murdered those they regarded as traitors, and that the government of the Republic of Ireland was unable to control the PIRA. He also alleged that the government of the Republic of Ireland would prosecute him as a former member of the PIRA.[17]

The Board of Immigration Appeals had held that, if extradition is refused as a result of a determination that the accused is sought for a political offense, he may not thereafter be deported to the requesting state, at least in the absence of assurances that he will not be prosecuted for such offense. However, the board found denial of extradition does not establish that the person is entitled to remain in the United States and that he may be deportable to another state.

The difficulties of using United States deportation procedures as an alternative to extradition should not be exaggerated. United States law grants substantial discretion to immigration authorities. The Immigration Service may disregard the alien's designated choice of country if it concludes that deportation to this country would be prejudicial to the interests of the United States.[18] Equally important, United States law provides that the prohibitions on deporting an alien to a country where his "life or freedom would be threatened in such country on account of race, religion, nationality, membership in a particular social group, or political opinion" do not apply if the attorney general determines that:

> (A) the alien ordered, incited, assisted, or otherwise participated in the persecution of any person on account of race, religion, nationality, membership in a particular social group, or political opinion;
>
> (B) the alien, having been convicted by final judgment of a particularly serious crime, constitutes a danger to the community of the United States;
>
> (C) there are serious reasons for considering that the alien has committed a serious nonpolitical crime outside the United States prior to the arrival of the alien in the United States; or
>
> (D) there are reasonable grounds for regarding the alien as a danger to the security of the United States.[19]

It is noteworthy also that there are over 700 different grounds for deportation,[20] and deportation is not barred where criminal proceedings are possible, or even probable, in the state of destination, unless the prosecution would be for a political crime.

The United States Supreme Court has recently concluded that the burden on a deportable alien to bar his deportation remains considerable. In *INS v. Stevic*,[21] the Court confirmed that, even as amended by the Refugee Act of 1980, the Immigration and Nationality Act requires a deportable alien to demonstrate a clear probability of persecution in order to obtain relief under section 243(H). The Court reversed the U.S. Court of Appeals for the Second Circuit, which had held that the Refugee Act of 1980 had changed the standard of proof that an alien must satisfy to obtain such relief and had substituted a "well founded fear of persecution" as the standard.

In determining whether an alien has committed a "serious nonpolitical crime" the Board of Immigration Appeals has relied on the *Handbook on Procedures and Criteria for Determining Refugee Status* (1979), published by the Office of the United Nations High Commissioner for Refugees.[22] The *Handbook* suggests that a "serious nonpolitical crime" must be "a capital crime or a very grave punishable act." At the same time the *Handbook* would balance the nature of the crime committed and the degree of persecution feared.

Dean Griffith has described the *Handbook's* approach to determining whether a crime is political as follows:

> In determining whether the crime is political or non-political, some consideration must be given to the motive behind its commission. If the crime is to be characterized as political, there should be a direct connection between the crime and the purported political objectives . . . The political aspect of the offense should also outweigh its common law character. It would be difficult,

however, to appreciate the political nature of the crime if it involved acts that were particularly cruel or repulsive. In any event, all the circumstances surrounding a particular act should be taken into account in determining whether a crime is non-political.[23]

An alien is entitled under United States law to request asylum during exclusion or deportation proceedings. Asylum requests made after exclusion or deportation proceedings have begun are treated as requests to withhold exclusion or deportation.[24]

Selected Foreign Countries

The pattern of law and procedures in foreign countries regarding exclusion and deportation varies considerably, and often involves a complex mixture of the Convention and Protocol Regarding the Status of Refugees, domestic constitutions and statutes, and regulations. For example, although Australia has acceded to both the convention and the protocol, its parliament has not enacted the legislation necessary to give these instruments the force of internal law.[25] Nor has the Australian parliament enacted a statutory procedure covering the granting of asylum. Nonetheless, as a policy matter, the Australian government grants asylum to all convention refugees. Applications for asylum are referred to a Committee for the Determination of Refugee Status before a final decision is rendered by the Ministry of Immigration and Ethnic Affairs.

Similarly, no Austrian statute guarantees the right of refugees under the convention not to be deported to countries where they are likely to be subject to persecution.[26] However, protection from extradition for purposes of prosecution or punishment on account of race, religion, nationality, or political opinion is guaranteed by statute, and this serves as a guide by analogy in deportation cases.

Moreover, an especially noteworthy provision of the new Austrian Law on extradition and Mutual Assistance in Criminal Matters is its explicit prohibition of utilizing deportation as a method for circumventing extradition.[27] This prohibition applies even prior to the filing of a formal request for extradition. If Austrian authorities encounter a fugitive whose extradition to a foreign state appears warranted, they are barred from employing methods of rendition other than extradition. This is considered to be part of the due process rights accorded to fugitives.

Belgium has not only enacted as domestic law the texts of both the convention and the protocol; it has also gone so far as to delegate to the representative of the United Nations High Commissioner for Refugees in Belgium the task of determining which persons are convention refugees.[28]

The constitution of Brazil declares that political refugees may not be extradited, and domestic regulation defines a political crime as including an attempt against the life of a head of state or other person a position of authority, anarchy, terrorism, sabotage, distribution of war propaganda, and any other action against the political or social order.[29] This broad definition of a political crime is narrowed under regulatory provisions which declare that no crime which is a major violation of ordinary criminal law shall be deemed a political offense and that no offense is political if it is committed in conjunction with an "ordinary crime" when such ordinary crime is the principal offense. Regulations also provide that no person may be deported for remaining in Brazil beyond the length of time permitted by his visa when such deportation would amount to an impermissible extradition. Accordingly, in some circumstances, the question of refugee status may be resolved in deportation proceedings.

France, the Federal Republic of Germany, and Italy all have provisions in their constitutions guaranteeing the right to asylum.[30] Each of these countries also has procedures whereby a refugee threatened by expulsion or deportation may challenge such an order. Other countries, not parties to the convention and the protocol, do not admit or grant asylum to refugees.[31] In such countries, refugees are given no special recognition.

The Netherlands is a special case.[32] Under article 66 of the Netherlands' constitution, the convention and the protocol automatically enjoy binding force and prevail over any legislation to the contrary.[33] The task of enforcing these provisions is assigned by domestic legislation to the Ministry of Justice. This legislation also specifically provides that refugees cannot be excluded or deported to a country where they fear persecution for reasons of religion, nationality, political opinion, or membership in a particular social group or race.

Illegal Methods of Rendition: Abduction and Unlawful Seizure

In this section we consider illegal or irregular methods of rendition. Abduction or kidnapping is the classic example. Another is the use of blackmail or other inducement or pressure on an accused to return to the country where he is wanted on criminal charges. Such measures may be undertaken by agents of states seeking return of an accused or by individuals acting on an individual basis. In other instances, irregular recovery may be accomplished by active cooperation between officials of the state seeking return and those of the territorial state or, at a minimum, passive cooperation or acquiesence by the territorial state to the irregular procedures employed.

Perhaps the best known case of abduction is the Israeli kidnapping of Adolf Eichmann from Argentina. Upon Argentina's complaint, the United Nations Security Council suggested Israel "make appropriate reparation" to Argentina "in accordance with the Charter of the United Nations and the rules of international law."[34] The matter was resolved by a joint communiqué in which Argentina and Israel noted the action taken by citizens of Israel infringed the fundamental rights of the state of Argentina.

More apposite to international terrorism is the case of Faik Bulut.[35] In February, 1972, during an Israel raid 100 miles into Lebanon, Bulut, a citizen of Turkey, was seized from a Palestinian refugee camp and taken into Israel by Israeli forces. When in Israel, Bulut was tried and convicted by an Israeli military court of the offense of belonging to Al-Fatah (a "terrorist" organization in Israel's perception) in Lebanon and Syria, and was sentenced to seven years in prison. In response to contentions by defense counsel that the statute and its application violated international law, the court cited the protective principle of criminal jurisdiction in upholding the statute and ruled that Bulut's involuntary abduction from Lebanon without extradition did not preclude jurisdiction. The legality of the Israeli action is highly questionable; some regard it as an especially egregious example of exorbitant criminal jurisdiction.[36]

As Professor Bassiouni has pointed out, abduction by the agents of one state in the territory of another may involve three distinct violations of law: "(a) disruption of world public order; (b) infringement on the sovereignty and territorial integrity of another state; and (c) violation of the human rights of the individual unlawfully seized."[37] Violations (b) and (c) were particularly at issue in the case of *United States v. Toscanino*.[38] There, the defendant, Francisco Toscanino, a citizen of Italy, was charged, with four others, with conspiracy to import narcotics into the United States. Upon appeal from a conviction, Toscanino contended that the court had acquired jurisdiction over him unlawfully through the conduct of U.S. agents. Specifically, he charged that he was abducted in Uruguay by members of the Montevideo police force in the pay of the United States government, and driven to the Uruguay-Brazil border, where he was picked up by Brazilians with the connivance of the United States government. According to Toscanino, he was then incessantly tortured and interrogated for seventeen days. During this time, United States government officials were allegedly aware of the interrogations and indeed, at times, a U.S. government official was present at them. Finally, Toscanino alleged, he was taken to Rio de Janeiro, drugged by Brazilian and U.S. agents, and placed on a plane to the United States in the custody of U.S. agents.

In challenging the jurisdiction of the court, Toscanino was faced with the obstacle of the so-called "Ker-Frisbie" doctrine, based on two United States Supreme Court cases which had held that the due process clause of the Fifth Amendment to the Constitution was limited to the right to a fair trial and did not apply to the methods used to obtain custody of an accused.[39] The Court of Appeals for the Second Circuit, however, held that the "Ker-Frisbie" doctrine had to be reconsidered in the context of subsequent Supreme Court decisions which had expanded the concept of due process and which protected an accused against pre-trial illegality by denying the government the fruits of any deliberate and unlawful activity on its part. The Second Circuit held further that a federal court must "divest itself from jurisdiction over the person of a defendant where it has been acquired as a result of the government's deliberate, unnecessary, and unreasonable invasion of the accused's constitutional rights."[40] By way of dicta, the court also indicated that the defendant could raise as a defense to jurisdiction that his abduction violated international treaties to which the United States was a party, specifically, the United Nations Charter and the Charter of the Organization of American States.

The Second Circuit remanded the case back to the district court for the purpose of determining whether Toscanino would be able to prove his allegations. After a hearing, the district court found that Toscanino had failed to meet his burden.[41]

Moreover, later court decisions have sharply narrowed the scope of *Toscanino*,[42] and at least one circuit court has expressly rejected it.[43] For example, in *United States ex rel Lujan v. Gengler*, the Second Circuit held that for a federal court to divest itself of jurisdiction, United States agents' actions outside the United States in obtaining custody over an accused must be "conduct of the most outrageous and reprehensible kind" that amounts to a denial of due process.[44] In *Lujan* the court found the government's conduct did not reach this level. The court also noted that neither Argentina (the state of nationality) nor Bolivia (the territorial state) had protested Lujan's abduction, and thus Lujan's allegation that his abduction violated the United Nations and OAS Charters could not be entertained. In the court's view Lujan's rights were strictly derivative and dependent upon a state's protesting a violation of its sovereignty. Acquiescence by the state whose sovereignty has been violated "waives any right it possessed and heals any violation of international law."[45]

Similarly, in *United States v. Lira,* the Second Circuit refused to apply *Toscanino* to a situation where there is no evidence of any gross misconduct on the part of United States agents.[46] In the court's view, its jurisdiction was not impaired by the alleged forceful abduction and torture of the accused by Chilean police.

Also of relevance is the Ninth Circuit's decision in *United States v. Valot*.[47] There the accused violated his parole obligation to the District of Hawaii by traveling to Asia, and a warrant was issued for his arrest. In 1977, Valot was arrested in Thailand on a marijuana charge and jailed; on May 4, 1979, Thai immigration officials brought Valot to the Bangkok airport, where he was turned over to U.S. Drug Enforcement Agency officials who, over his protest, took him aboard a flight to Honolulu. Valot contended, *inter alia*, that his removal from Thailand violated the extradition treaty between the United States and Thailand and that this violation barred his prosecution.

The Ninth Circuit rejected this contention. According to the court, where no demand for extradition is made by the United States and the defendant is deported by the authority of the other country which is party to the treaty, no "extradition" has taken place. There was, therefore, no need to comply with the extradition treaty.

In the same vein, the Court in *United States v. Cordero* stated that

> The short and conclusive answer to appellant's claim, however, is that nothing in these treaties suggests that the countries involved must follow the procedures set out in the treaties when they return criminal defendants to the United States. Extradition treaties normally consist of commitments between governments to the effect that each will return those accused of certain crimes at the request of the other . . . Nothing in the treaty prevents a sovereign nation from deporting foreign nationals for other reasons and in other ways should it wish to do so.[48]

Professor Bassiouni, in discussing three other cases involving pleas of an unlawful seizure, has pointed out

> Interestingly enough, in these three cases the judicial authorities have never been involved, nor were they advised of the cases, nor did they have an opportunity to intervene. Cooperation in all these cases was between law enforcement authorities who avoided and evaded judicial and legal processes. These cases may point to a trend in extradition practices where police work out their own arrangements to obtain rendition of individuals irrespective of what the legal system requires, and in avoidance of the judicial authorities altogether. This creates, of course, serious problems for the integrity of the legal process, even though it may be a manifestation of the frustration of law enforcement authorities with their inability to make the extradition system work with the speed and satisfaction they desire.[49]

Professor Bassiouni noted further that United States courts have ruled that evidence secured by torture of an accused abroad has been admitted in United States proceedings if United States officials were in no way engaged in the torture. This position would change, Bassiouni suggests, were the United Nations to adopt a Draft Convention on the Prevention and Suppression of Torture currently pending before it and were the United States to become a party to the convention.

Further with respect to the human rights dimensions of forcible abduction or other means of irregular rendition, Tentative Draft Number 3 of the Restatement of Foreign Relations Law of the United States (Revised) states:

> None of the international human rights conventions to date . . . has expressly provided that forcible abduction or irregular extradition is a violation of in-

ternational human rights law, but Articles 3, 5, and 9 of the Universal Declaration of Human Rights as well as Articles 7, 9 and 10 of the International Covenant on Civil and Political Rights might be invoked in support of such a view. In 1981, a Human Rights Committee established pursuant to Article 28 of the Covenant decided that the abduction of a Uruguayan refugee from Argentina by Uruguayan security officers constituted an arbitrary arrest and detention in violation of Article 9(1) . . .[50]

As indicated by the above discussion, the "Ker-Frisbie" doctrine largely retains its full vitality, both in the United States and abroad. Consequently, in the absence of any move toward change in the doctrine, one may expect law enforcement officials to continue to resort to abduction and other illegal measures of rendition — clearly this is likely in cases where extradition or other legal methods of rendition are unavailable and perhaps, increasingly, even in cases where they are.

Notes

1. Evans, "The Apprehension and Prosecution of Offenders," in A. E. Evans and J. F. Murphy, eds., *Legal Aspects of International Terrorism* (1978) p. 493.
2. Evans, "Obtaining People and Evidence from Abroad Through Formal Legal Processes," in R. Lillich, *International Aspects of Criminal Law: Enforcing United States Law in the World Community* (1981), pp. 1, 2.
3. Evans, supra note 1, at 494.
4. Convention Relating to the Status of Refugees, done July 28, 1951, 189 U.N.T.S. 137, entered into force, Apr. 22, 1954.
5. Protocol Relating to the Status of Refugees, done January 31, 1967, 19 U.S.T. 6223, T.I.A.S. No. 6577, 606 U.N.T.S. 267, entered into force Oct. 4, 1967.
6. See Protocol, preamble and art. I, para. 2.
7. I. M. C. Bassiouni, *International Extradition: United States Law and Practice* vol. IV, §3-3-3-11 (1983).
8. Warbrick, *Irregular Extradition, 1983 Public Law*: 269.
9. Id., at 275.
10. Id., at 276.
11. At least this has been the case with respect to the deportation of hijackers of civil aircraft. See table 1-2 set forth in Evans, *Aircraft and Aviation Facilities*, in A. E. Evans and J. F. Murphy, eds., *Legal Aspects of International Terrorism*, 3, 17 (1978).
12. See M. C. Bassiouni, supra note 7, at IV, §2-4.
13. Quimones v. Kennedy, 374 U.S. 469 (1963).
14. See M. C. Bassiouni, supra note 7, at IV, §2-5.
15. See, generally, 8 U.S.C. §1252, (1976 and Supp. 1984). Woodby v. INS, 385 U.S. 276 (1966).
16. M. C. Bassiouni, supra note 7, at IV, §2-8.
17. McMullen v. Immigration and Naturalization Service, 658 F.2d 1312 (9th Cir. 1981).
18. 8 U.S.C. §1253(a) (1976 and Supp. 1984).
19. 8 U.S.C. §1253(h) (1976 and Supp. 1984).
20. M. C. Bassiouni, supra note 7, at IV, §2-8-2-9.
21. — — — U.S. — — —, 81 L. ed. 2nd 321, 104 S.CT. 2489 (1984).
22. In re Rodriguez-Palma, Int. Dec. No. 2185 (BIA Aug. 26, 1980).
23. Griffith, "Deportation and the Refugee,," *1983 Michigan Yearbook of International Legal Studies: Transnational Legal Problems of Refugees*, 125, 136, fn. 53.
24. 8 CFR §§108.3(a) and (b) (1980).

25. This description of Australian law is taken from "Review of Foreign Laws," Appendix III, in *1983 Michigan Yearbook of International Legal Studies*, supra note 23, at 553–54.
26. E. Palmer, *The Austrian Law on Extradition and Mutual Assistance in Criminal Matters*, 57 (1983).
27. Id., at 32.
28. *Michigan Yearbook*, supra note 25, at 557–58.
29. Id., at 558–60.
30. Id., at 564–66, 566–70, and 571–73.
31. For example, the Philippines and Singapore. See id., at 578–79 (Philippines) and at 579–80 (Singapore).
32. Id., at 575–77.
33. Article 66 of the Netherlands constitution provides:

Legislation which is in force within the Kingdom shall not be applied if its application would be incompatible with provisions of agreements which are binding upon everyone whether such agreements have been entered into before or after the enactment of the legislation.

34. S.C. Res. 4349 (June 23, 1960).
35. For a discussion of this incident, see note, "Extraterritorial Jurisdiction and Jurisdiction Following Forcible Abduction: A New Israel Precedent in International Law," *Michigan Law Review* 72 (1974): 1087, 1088.
36. Id.
37. See M. C. Bassiouni, supra note 7, at V §2-1.
38. 500 F.2d 267 (2d Cir. 1974).
39. Ker v. Illinois, 119 U.S. 436 (1888); Frisbie v. Collins, 342 U.S. 519 (1952).
40. 500 F.2d at 275.
41. 398 F. Supp. 916 (E.D.N.Y. 1975).
42. See, e.g., United States v. Lara, 539 F.2d 495 (5th Cir. 1976) (forcible abduction does not necessarily involve Toscanino Rule "even if that principle did apply in this Circuit"); United States v. Lira, 515 F.2d 68 (2d cir. 1975) (no direct U.S. involvement where United States asked for expulsion from Chile). See also United States v. Marzano, 388 F. Supp. 906 (N.D. Ill. 1975) (removal from Grand Canyon is not abduction although U.S. agents paid the fare and accompanied defendants; existence of an extradition treaty was not relevant).
43. United States v. Herrera, 504 F.2d 859 (5th Cir. 1975), cert denied, 421 U.S. 1001 (1975).
44. 510 F.2d 62 (2nd Cir.), cert. denied, 421 U.S. 1001 (1975).
45. Id., at 67.
46. 515 F.2d 68 (2d Cir. 1975).
47. 625 F.2d 308 (9th Cir. 1980).
48. 668 F.2d 32, 37 (1st Cir. 1981).
49. M. C. Bassiouni, supra note 7, at V, §3-5.
50. American Law Institute, *Restatement of Foreign Relations Law of the United States (Revised), Tentative Draft No. 3* §432, reporters' note 1, at 42.

CHAPTER 4

International Judicial Assistance in Criminal Matters

The term "international judicial assistance" may be broadly defined to include arrangements between states for the exchange of information regarding criminal investigations, service of documents, interrogation of witnesses, transfer of criminal proceedings, enforcement of criminal judgments, and transfer and supervision of offenders convicted in the other country. In Western Europe, arrangements for judicial assistance in criminal matters are well developed. Until recently, however, the United States has not been involved in international agreements on judicial assistance with regard to criminal matters.

International judicial assistance takes on particular importance in connection with the extradite or prosecute obligation contained in the multilateral, antiterrorist conventions to which the United States is a party. If the United States decides not to extradite an alleged offender to the requesting country, it is obliged, as we have seen in earlier chapters, to submit the accused for the purpose of prosecution. But this obligation lacks meaningful content if the United States has no procedural means of obtaining the evidence necessary to ensure conviction of the accused in consonance with due process and other constitutional protections afforded by United States law.

As Michael Tigar and Austin Doyle have pointed out:

> Obtaining information from abroad in criminal cases poses many of the same problems as obtaining the defendant himself. The parallels are, with only slight exaggeration, simply stated. A treaty that imposes reciprocal obligations upon the signatories to render requested data is analogous to an extradition treaty. Deportation resembles the unilateral decision of a foreign sovereign to send data out of the country to a particular place. Defendants are sometimes kidnapped across international frontiers, and information is some-

times obtained by means beneath the law, often without the consent of the sovereign from whose territory the information is taken.[1]

The problems do not necessarily end once the information is obtained. Then the issue of its admissibility at trial may arise.

To illustrate the difficulties in obtaining evidence from abroad for the purpose of prosecuting alleged terrorists, and the issue of the admissibility of such evidence at trial, we first explore international judicial assistance in United States law and practice. Then we briefly examine the experience in Austria as an example of the Western European approach for comparative and contrastive purposes and as a possible model for reform in the United States.

United States Law and Experience

There is, of course, a substantial amount of informal exchange of information regarding criminal matters among law enforcement officials of various countries. Such exchanges are facilitated by the International Criminal Police Organization (Interpol), of which the United States, along with various other countries, is a member. Interpol has been of only limited utility, however, with respect to combating international terrorism because its constitution provides in article 3 that it is "strictly forbidden for the organization to undertake any intervention or activities of a political, military, religious or social character." As a consequence, Interpol has proceeded cautiously in its involvement with law enforcement agencies combating terrorism. Interpol will not involve itself in intelligence activity aimed at preventing terrorist acts; however, once a terrorist act has occurred, it will assist in law enforcement efforts and at apprehending individuals responsible. This policy also has led Interpol to include in its files only those individuals who are directly implicated in a crime. Those individuals only suspected of involvement in terrorist activity are excluded.[2]

This stage does not, of course, involve international *judicial* assistance since it takes place before apprehension of the alleged offender. The problems often become increasingly complex after apprehension.

For example, foreign policemen, not subject to the privilege against self-incrimination, may interrogate a suspect in a manner and for a duration that would not be permitted in the United States. Or foreign law enforcement officials may engage in a warrantless search that would not be permitted under United States law. At trial in the United States defense counsel may object that any evidence obtained through such activities by foreign law enforcement officials should be excluded. United States courts have held, however, that such evidence will be admitted unless United States officials themselves participate along with the foreign law enforcement officials.[3] According to these decisions, both the Fourth Amendment's ban on unreasonable search and seizure and the exclusionary rule are designed to deter the unconstitutional actions of United States law enforcement officials only.[4] On the other hand, at least one case has held the Fourth Amendment applicable to surveillance of United States citizens abroad by foreign officials if such surveillance was suggested by United States officials.[5]

Further, when taking testimony abroad through depositions, it is important to assure that an accused's Sixth Amendment right to confront witnesses against him is preserved.

There may also be formidable difficulties in obtaining the evidence abroad at all, because of the attitude of the state in which the evidence is located. Civil law countries may be especially sensitive to the intrusion of foreign evidence-gathering agencies.[6] The use of letters rogatory, a basic United States method of obtaining evidence abroad for use in criminal proceedings in the United States, poses a number of practical problems. These include, for example, a lack of specified procedures for taking testimonial evidence in the requested country or of mandatory procedures regarding authentication of foreign public documents, and the discretionary nature of the process and lack of specification of grounds for denying execution of letters rogatory.[7] As a result of these and other problems, the United States has recently been actively engaged in negotiating mutual assistance treaties in criminal matters.[8]

The first major international agreement that the United States entered into for the purpose of obtaining information and evidence needed for criminal investigation and prosecutions was the 1973 Treaty on Mutual Assistance in Criminal Matters with Switzerland, which entered into force January 23, 1977.[9] The treaty provides for assistance in locating the whereabouts of witnesses, taking of testimony, service of judicial and administrative orders, and authentication of records; and it makes special provision for assistance in covering organized crime. Its principal purpose is to facilitate the acquisition of relevant information about crime and the building of a case against the accused. The treaty exempts from investigation, however, any offenses that the requested state deems to be political in nature or connected therewith unless offenses can be ascribed to an organized criminal group that uses violence as one of its techniques of actions.[10] There is, accordingly, a need to ensure that terrorist activity will not be deemed by a requested state to be political in nature.

More recent agreements have extended the parameters of the United States–Swiss Treaty. A treaty between the United States and Italy, for example, covers such assistance in criminal investigations and proceedings as:

    a. locating persons;
    b. serving documents;

c. producing documents and records;
d. executing requests for search and seizure;
e. taking testimony;
f. transferring persons in custody for testimonial purposes; and
g. immobilizing and forfeiting assets.

Other types of assistance shall also be granted to the extent such assistance is not inconsistent with the law of the Requested State.[11]

The treaty also requires assistance "even when the acts under investigation are not offenses in the Requested State and without regard to whether the Requested State would have jurisdiction in similar circumstances."[12]

With respect to taking testimony, the treaty provides in pertinent part that

3. The Requested State shall permit the presence of an accused, counsel for the accused, and persons charged with the enforcement of the criminal laws to which the request relates.

4. The executing authority shall provide persons permitted to be present the opportunity to question the person whose testimony is sought in accordance with the laws of the Requested State.

5. The executing authority shall provide persons permitted to be present the opportunity to propose additional questions and other investigative measures.[13]

These provisions would seem to ensure that the Sixth Amendment's right of an accused to be confronted with witnesses against him will be protected in a requested state. They also specify the procedures for taking testimonial evidence in the requested country and thus resolve a problem that often obtains in the absence of a mutual assistance treaty. Other provisions of the treaty similarly resolve problems that often arise in attempting to obtain evidence from abroad in the absence of a treaty.[14]

The treaty, however, does not come to grips with the problem most relevant to the prosecution and punishment of international terrorists, namely, the political offense exception. On the contrary, the treaty provides that the requested state may deny assistance if "a request relates to a purely military offense or a matter considered a political offense by the Requested State."[15] Nowhere does the treaty provide for the exclusion of terrorist offenses from the political offense category.

The United States–Turkey Treaty on Extradition and Mutual Assistance in Criminal Matters goes one step still further and excludes from the political offense exception to the obligation to render judicial assistance: "(a) Offenses for which investigations and proceedings are obligatory for the Contracting Parties under multilateral international agreements; and (b) Offenses against a Head of State or a Head of Government or members of their families."[16] The multilateral international agreements referred to in this provision include, most particularly, the antiterrorist conventions.

It has traditionally been easier for foreign states to obtain evidence in the United States for purposes of criminal prosecution than it has been for the United States to obtain evidence abroad. Several court decisions have held that 28 U.S.C. §1782 applies to criminal as well as civil matters for which evidence is sought.[17]

Nonetheless, a special problem in this connection arose during the 1970s in the case of the Lockheed Aircraft Corporation's and other corporate payments of millions of dollars in bribes to officials or political figures in Asia, Europe, and Latin America in connection with military and commercial contracts.[18] As a result of revelations in Congress of such payments, numerous governments requested access to information regarding alleged payoffs to their officials from the Department of State, the Department of Justice, the Securities and Exchange Commission, Senate committees, and even the comptroller general. Existing United States federal law deals solely with the power of the judiciary to render assistance to foreign tribunals and was therefore simply inapplicable to these requests. To resolve the many problems raised by these requests, the United States entered into executive agreements with a number of countries specifying the terms under which information could be supplied to them. These agreements were concluded on an ad hoc basis with reference to a particular subject of criminal investigation. United States law, however, still does not generally cover requests for information in criminal cases that are presented outside of the judiciary. To meet the need for greater scope, Bruno Ristau, formerly Director of the Office of Foreign Litigation, Department of Justice, has proposed a federal statute that would confer on the attorney general permanent authority to render assistance to foreign law enforcement agencies in the investigation and prosecution of offenses.[19]

Another type of judicial assistance agreement was concluded between the United States and Mexico on November 25, 1976.[20] This treaty on the execution of prison sentences has enabled the national of one state who is a prisoner in the other state to return to his own state to serve his sentence. No exchange is to be made, however, where a prisoner is serving time for "a political offense within the meaning of the Treaty of Extradition of 1899 between the parties, nor an offense under the immigration or the purely military laws of a party."[21] A similar treaty was concluded with Canada on March 2, 1977.[22] The constitutionality of these treaties has recently been confirmed by United States courts.[23]

Despite these developments, it is safe to conclude that the United States is still insufficiently involved internationally in efforts to extend the development and use of various methods of judicial assistance. In this regard states in Western Europe are substantially ahead of the United States. Their accomplishments may serve as a guide for further efforts, although admittedly the peculiar aspects of United States laws of evidence regarding admissibility present a substantial barrier to more extended United States initiatives in this area.

The Western European Experience: A Glance at Austria

The subject of international judicial assistance and cooperation in criminal matters in Western Europe has been treated in magisterial fashion elsewhere,[24] and this section makes no attempt to replicate those treatments. Suffice it for present purposes to take a brief look at the law and practice in Austria, a country where mutual judicial assistance in criminal matters plays an important role. Austria's law on mutual judicial assistance is found in regional and bilateral conventions and in federal statutes.[25]

Austria is dependent, as are most European legal systems, on mutual assistance in criminal matters because its criminal jurisdiction extends to many offenses committed outside of its territory. Moreover, under the Austrian and other European systems of procedure, most acts of investigation are carried out by governmental officials rather than private parties, and evidence procured by means of mutual assistance is generally admissible in trials under the law of evidence.

Austrian law does not define mutual assistance, or list the types of acts falling within its scope, in order not to limit the development of new forms of assistance. Under Austrian practice, forms of assistance include the giving of information by Austrian authorities; the service of summonses; the carrying out of investigative acts such as the interrogation of witnesses and the accused, searches, and seizures; the transmitting of records and property; and the temporary transfer of a person, for evidentiary purposes, to a requesting state. New forms of cooperation in this area include the transfer of criminal proceedings, the supervision of a person conditionally sentenced or released by a foreign court, and the enforcement of foreign criminal judgments.

A significant limitation of Austrian law on mutual assistance is that imposed on the nature of the requesting authority. Usually, only requests of courts and public prosecutors will be considered, and those of administrative agencies only when they are involved in the enforcement of a sentence. Austria renders assistance in police investigations within the context of Interpol and has agreements with the Federal Republic of Germany, Italy, and Switzerland, supplemental to the European Mutual Assistance Convention, that provide for such assistance.

Other limitations under Austrian law on the giving of mutual assistance include a requirement of double criminality, except for the service of a process to a willing recipient; exceptions for political, military, and fiscal offenses; a requirement that the foreign proceeding and enforcement live up to the due process requirements of the European Human Rights Convention; and considerations of secrecy and privileged communications.

There are a few provisions of Austrian law that relate to particular acts of assistance. For example, a foreign summons which threatens coercive measures to enforce appearance will only be served in Austria if it is coupled with an instruction that these measures are unenforceable there. Further as a condition to service of a summons, the requesting state must guarantee safe conduct with regard to offenses committed by the summoned person prior to his departure from Austria. This safe conduct does not, however, cover an offense with which the accused is charged and for which he is summoned to attend his trial; nor does it extend to offenses committed by the summoned person after leaving Austria. There is also a requirement that safe conduct be guaranteed for the temporary transfer of a person under detention in Austria to a requesting state that wishes his presence for investigative acts.

An important limitation on the interrogation of witnesses is the lack of cross-examination. Under Austria's inquisitorial procedure, the judge governs the taking of evidence and interrogates the witness. Although the prosecutor, the accused, and his defender may question the witness directly after the presiding judge has given them permission to do so, a cross-examination as it is known in Anglo-American procedure is simply not possible.

Austrian law, in accordance with the Western European approach, generally provides that foreign officials may not carry out acts of investigation or procedural acts in Austrian territory. Nonetheless, a new law allows foreign officials to be present and to participate in acts of mutual assistance, such as interrogations that are conducted by Austrian authorities. Such presence and participation of foreign officials requires in each instance a special permit from the Austrian federal minister of justice. Austrian law also permits foreign counsel to be present and participate in investigative acts, without the permission of the federal minister of justice. Article 6 of the European Human Rights Convention, to which Austria is a party, requires the presence of foreign counsel in pretrial testimony, and safe conduct is granted to entering foreign counsel, foreign officials, and other participants in the proceedings for offenses committed prior to entry.

* * * *

Alona Evans has aptly summarized the importance of international judicial assistance in combating international terrorism:

> Extended development and use of various methods of judicial assistance will hardly solve all the problems involved in the apprehension and prosecution of

international terrorists. But these methods can serve not only to supplement present lawful means of apprehension and prosecution in practical terms, but more importantly, they may contribute to the development of a positive climate in which such controls of international terrorism can be effectively undertaken. That is, judicial assistance can help to reduce one state's suspicion of another's motives for requesting rendition of an offender or one state's suspicion of another's standards of criminal procedure and penology. Both views inhibit mutual cooperation in carrying out international obligations with regard to the control of international terrorism.[26]

Notes

1. Tigar and Doyle, "International Exchange of Information in Criminal Cases," *Michigan Yearbook of International Legal Studies, Transnational Aspects of Criminal Procedure,* p. 61.
2. See, generally, Kerstetter, "Practical Problems of Law Enforcement," in A. E. Evans and J. F. Murphy, eds., *Legal Aspects of International Terrorism* (1978), p. 535.
3. See e.g., Brulay v. United States, 383 F.2d 345 (9th Cir.) cert.denied, 389 U.S. 986 (1967); Rosado v. Civiletti, 621 F.2d 1179 (2d Cir. 1980).
4. For a discussion of these and other points, *see* Saltzburg, "The Reach of the Bill of Rights Beyond the Terra Firma of the United States," in R. Lillich, ed., *International Aspects of Criminal Law: Enforcing United States Law in the World Community* (1981), p. 107.
5. United States v. Jordan, 233 C.M.A. 525, 50 C.M.R. 664 (1975), modified, 24 C.M.A. 156, 51 C.M.R. 375 (1976).
6. See, e.g., Chamblee, "International Legal Assistance in Criminal Cases," in ABA National Institute, *Transnational Litigation: Practical Approaches to Conflicts and Accommodations,* vol. 1 (1984).
7. See Abbell, "International Assistance in Criminal Investigations and Prosecutions," *Extraterritorial Discovery in International Litigation* (PLI 1984): pp. 227, 231.
8. See Chamblee, supra note 6, at 219-32.
9. 1973 Treaty on Mutual Assistance in Criminal Matters with Switzerland, May 25, 1973, United States-Switzerland, 27 U.S.T. 2019; T.I.A.S. No. 8302.
10. Art. 2(1)(c)(1).
11. On June 28, 1984, the Senate gave its advice and consent to ratification of the Mutual Legal Assistance Treaty with Italy, and the president ratified the treaty on Aug. 10, 1984. The quoted language may be found in art. 1(2) of the Treaty.
12. Id., art 1(3).
13. Id., art. 15(3)(4)(5).
14. See, e.g., id., arts. 16, 17, 18.
15. Id., art 5(1)(b).
16. Treaty on Extradition and Mutual Assistance in Criminal Matters, June 7, 1979, United States-Turkey, T.I.A.S. No. 9891, entered into force Jan. 1, 1981. Art. 22(2)(a)(b).
17. In re Letters Rogatory From the Justice Court, District of Montreal, Canada, 523 F.2d 562 (6th Cir. 1975); In re Letters Rogatory from Tokyo District, 539 F.2d 1216 (9th Cir. 1976).
18. See Ristau, "International Cooperation in Penal Matters: The 'Lockheed Agreements,'" in *1983 Michigan Yearbook of International Legal Studies,* supra note 1, at 85.
19. Id., at 97-98.
20. Treaty on the Execution of Penal Sentences, signed at Mexico, Nov. 25, 1976, United States-Mexico, 28 U.S.T. 7399; T.I.A.S. No. 8718, entered into force Nov. 30, 1977.
21. Id., art. II (4).
22. Treaty on the Execution of Penal Sentences, Mar. 2, 1977, United States-Canada, 30 U.S.T. 6263; T.I.A.S. No. 9552, entered into force July 19, 1978.
23. Pfeifer v. U.S. Bureau of Prisons, 615 F.2d 873 (9th Cir. 1980), aff'd 468 F. Supp. 920 (S.D. Cal. 1979); Rosado v. Civiletti, 621 F.2d 1179 (2d Cir. 1980).

24. See Grützner, International Judicial Assistance and Cooperation in Criminal Matters, M. C. Bassiouni and V. Nanda, eds., *A Treatise on International Criminal Law*, vol. 2 (1973), p. 189.

25. This account of Austria's law on mutual judicial assistance is taken from E. Palmer, *The Austrian Law on Extradition and Mutual Assistance in Criminal Matters,* (1983), pp. 80-101.

26. Evans, "The Apprehension and Prosecution of Offenders: Some Current Problems," in A. E. Evans and J. F. Murphy, eds., *Legal Aspects of International Terrorism* (1978), pp. 493, 503.

PART TWO

Punishing International Terrorists: The Elusive Goal

CHAPTER 5

Apprehension, Prosecution, and Punishment of International Terrorists: State Practice

In undertaking to determine the extent to which international terrorists have actually been prosecuted and punished for their crimes, one is immediately struck by the paucity of available data. With the possible exception of aircraft hijacking or sabotage against civil aviation—where in the United States the Federal Aviation Administration (FAA) has compiled rather extensive statistics on this subject—neither governmental nor private sources have been much interested in the final fate of the international terrorist.

In the numerous reports compiled by the Office for Combating Terrorism, U.S. Department of State, for example, one finds statistics regarding, *inter alia*, the number of international terrorist incidents, their geographical distribution by category of event (kidnapping, bombing, and so on), death and injuries due to international terrorist attack, the type and nationality of the victim, and the names of terrorist groups throughout the world.[1] Very rarely, however, is there any mention of the arrest of an alleged terrorist, much less of his prosecution and punishment, and little of this information has been compiled on a sustained and systematic basis.

The same pattern seems to prevail when one turns to private sources of information regarding international terrorism. Private organizations that specialize in advising private businesses and individuals as to ways to avoid terrorism are apparently unconcerned with the prosecution and punishment of the international terrorist. The mass media, with some exceptions, tend to lose interest after the conclusion of a terrorist event, and if they report the arrest of an alleged terrorist, they rarely follow up with a story regarding his prosecution and punishment (if any).

Parenthetically, it is interesting to note that, even with respect to terrorism taking place solely within the United States and subject to the jurisdiction of the Federal Bureau of Investigation (FBI), there is little information available regarding the arrest, prosecution, and punishment of alleged terrorists. Although the FBI annually prepares an analysis of terrorist incidents in the United States,[2] seldom do these reports go beyond a description of the incident itself, the nature of the group or individual perpetrating it, and the extent of injury to persons or property. Somewhat more information regarding arrest and punishment is available in a report the FBI submits to the attorney general on its major accomplishments during the year regarding the combating of terrorism;[3] but here, too, the information provided is relatively incomplete and not the primary thrust of the FBI's report.

Accordingly, outside of the area of aircraft hijacking, and to some extent even within it, the report that follows is necessarily impressionistic and unsystematic, culled from a great variety of sources. It draws heavily from, attempts to build on, and owes a great debt of gratitude to the pioneering work done by Alona E. Evans.[4] Although the report can in no sense be described as exhaustive, the hope is that it will nonetheless provide a skeletal outline of state experience in apprehending, prosecuting, and punishing international terrorists and will serve as a helpful backdrop to the next chapter of this study on conclusions and recommendations for reform in law and practice.

Attacks Against Aircraft and Aviation Facilities

OVERVIEW

Before turning to the record of prosecution and punishment of those who attack aircraft and aviation facilities, it may be useful to have a brief overview of recent trends regarding the frequency of this form of criminal activity. According to a July 1982 report of the Office for Combating Terrorism, U.S. Department of State, there have been 684 attempted skyjackings since January 1968, with at least 500 deaths and 400 injuries resulting.[5] Of these 684 skyjacking attempts, 108 were considered to have been terrorist (that is, politically motivated). More than one-third of these resulted in casualties, with 212 dead and 186 wounded.

The high point in attempted skyjacking was reached in 1969–1970, with declines in 1971–1972 and 1973. The level of skyjacking activity remained fairly constant after that, although there was an increase in the early 1980s, due in part to a rash of skyjackings to Cuba by homesick Cuban refugees who utilized real or claimed flammable liquid as a weapon. Approximately 47 terrorist groups, of which almost half were Palestinian and Latin American, claimed responsibility for the skyjackings.

Sabotage, in the form of explosions aboard aircraft, was responsible for the deaths of 1,037 people between 1949 and 1982.[6] The high-water year appears to have been 1976, with five incidents and 168 people killed. Since that time the number of incidents and especially the number of persons killed have dropped sharply.

ENFORCEMENT OF LAWS AND REGULATIONS

With respect to obtaining custody over hijackers, continuing the practice noted earlier by Alona Evans,[7] the preferred methods continue to be exclusion and deportation. Indeed, from 1977 to 1982, the period covered by this study, formal extradition was granted only once, as compared with approximately 14 cases of exclusion or deportation.[8] In one other case, although extradition (to the USSR) was denied, the requested state (Sweden), prosecuted the hijacker and sentenced him to four years in prison. The disposition of a 1977 request from Bulgaria to Yugoslavia for the extradition of a hijacker is unknown. A summary of the methods of rendition of hijackers utilized during the 1977-1982 period, as well as the disposition of these cases, is set forth in Tables 5.1 and 5.2.

As Alona Evans found in 1977, "It is difficult to determine with any accuracy the total number of persons who have been apprehended in the period covered by the study or the disposition of their cases."[9] Nonetheless, at least with respect to persons involved in hijacking of United States registered aircraft, the data indicate rather widespread prosecution and conviction, and the imposition of severe penalties. For the persons involved in 72 hijackings during the 1977-1982 period, the range of sentences was from four months plus probation to life. The average sentence was 24 years, and the average sentence for air piracy or kidnapping was 30 years. A summary of the disposition of these cases is set forth in table 5.3. Table 5.4 is a summary of international hijackings from 1977 to 1982.

Overall, as reported by the FAA,[10] from January 9, 1969 through 1982, approximately 353 persons have been involved in 256 hijackings of United States–registered aircraft. Of these, 152 have been convicted for their crimes, 141 in the United States and 11 in foreign countries; 5 were acquitted; and 27 were assigned to mental institutions. In twenty cases the charges were dismissed or prosecution declined, and 23 hijackers were either killed or committed suicide during the hijack attempt. As of January 1, 1983, eleven cases were pending, and there were 115 fugitives, including a number of passive companions indicted along with the active hijackers.

It is interesting to note further that, since Professor Evans's study, there has been a substantial increase in the number of countries that have become parties to the relevant aviation convention. As of January 1, 1984, there were 117 parties to the Tokyo Convention, 121 to the Hague Convention and 119 to the Montreal Convention.[11] By contrast, as of June 30, 1977, the figures were 87 parties to the Tokyo Convention, 80 to the Hague Conven-

Table 5.1 Domestic and Foreign Aircraft Hijackings, 1977–1982

Year	Result	Flight Originating From	Hijackers Apprehended in	Registry	No. of Persons Apprehended	Disposition of Case
1977	S	Spain	Switzerland	Spanish	1	Sentenced by Swiss court to 10 yrs; failed to return from leave; apprehended in Italy; sentenced to 9 yrs.
1977	U	Japan	Japan	U.S.	1	Deported to U.S.; committed to mental institution; released after 18 mos.
1977	U	U.S.	England	U.S.	1	Excluded; returned; susp. sentence; psychiatric treatment
1977	S	USSR	Sweden	USSR	1	Extradition denied; sentenced by Swedish court to 4 yrs.
1977	S	Bulgaria	Yugoslavia	Bulgarian	1	Extradition requested in 8/77; result unknown
1977	S	Lebanon	Kuwait	Lebanese	1	Released on humanitarian grounds; to be deported to Lebanon
1977	S	Chile	Peru	Chile	4	Deported to Cuba for asylum
1977	S	USSR	Finland	USSR	2	Excluded from Finland; returned to USSR; sentences of 8 and 15 yrs.
1977	S	E. Germany	W. Germany	Czech	2	Sentenced by W. German court to 6 yrs. and 3.5 yrs.
1977	S	Spain	Somalia	W. German	4	Sentenced by Somali court to 20 yrs; sentenced in absentia by Italian court to 30 yrs. (3 killed)
1977	S	Vietnam	Singapore	Vietnamese	4	Sentenced to 14 yrs. by Singapore government
1978	S	E. Germany	W. Germany	Czech	1	Sentenced to 4 yrs. by W. German court
1978	U	Netherlands	Spain	Dutch	1	Extradited to Netherlands
1978	S	Poland	W. Germany	Polish	1	Sentenced by W. German court to 9 mos. for hostage taking (hijacker and 8 passengers sought political asylum)
1978	U	U.S.	Switzerland	U.S.	1	Excluded from Switzerland; sentenced in U.S. to 7 yrs. and 5 yrs. concurrently
1979	U	Norway	Sweden	USSR	3	Sentenced by Swedish court; two sentenced to 3 yrs., one to 18 mos.

Year	S/U	Origin	Destination	Nationality	N	Disposition
1979	S	Nicaragua	Costa Rica	Nicaraguan	3	Expelled to Panama
1979	S	U.S.	Ireland	U.S.	1	Deported to U.S.; sentenced to 40 yrs.
1979	U	Bangladesh	India	Bangladeshi	1	Returned to Bangladesh per Bangladesh government request of Indian officials
1979	S	Canary Islands	Switzerland	Spanish	3	Sentenced to 20 mos. by Swiss court (hijackers were Spanish Foreign Legion deserters seeking political asylum)
1979	U	Guatemala	U.S.	U.S.	1	Declared mentally incompetent by U.S. court; charges dropped
1979	S	Libya	Cyprus	Libyan	1	Turned over to Libyan delegation; executed in Libya
1979	S	U.S.	Mexico	U.S.	1	Deported to U.S.; sentenced to 16 mos.
1980	S	U.S.	Cuba	U.S.	2	Reportedly sentenced in Cuba to 5 yrs. and 4 yrs.
1980	S	U.S.	Cuba	U.S.	6	Reportedly sentenced in Cuba to terms ranging from 2 to 4 yrs.
1980	S	U.S.	Cuba	U.S.	4	Reportedly sentenced in Cuba to 2 yrs. then freed by judicial order
1980	S	Puerto Rico	Cuba	U.S.	1	Reportedly sentenced in Cuba to 4 yrs.
1980	S	U.S.	Cuba	U.S.	7	Reportedly sentenced in Cuba to 3 yrs.
1980	S	U.S.	Cuba	U.S.	3	Reportedly sentenced in Cuba to terms ranging from 2 to 3 yrs.
1980	S	U.S.	Cuba	U.S.	1	Reportedly sentenced in Cuba to 2 yrs.
1980	S	U.S.	Cuba	U.S.	2	Reportedly sentenced in Cuba to 4 yrs. and 3 yrs.
1980	S	U.S.	Cuba	U.S.	2	Excluded from Cuba; released to custody of U.S. Marshals; sentenced in U.S. to 40 yrs.
1980	U	Uruguay	Argentina	Uruguayan	1	Sentenced in Argentina to 11 yrs.
1980	S	Poland	W. Germany	Polish	1	Sentenced in Germany to 4 yrs.
1981	U	Turkey	Bulgaria	Turkish	4	Sentenced in Bulgaria to 3 yrs.
1981	S	U.S.	Cuba	U.S.	2	Reportedly sentenced in Cuba to 10 yrs.
1981	S	Poland	W. Germany	Polish	1	Sentenced in W. Germany to 5 yrs.
1981	S	Poland	W. Germany	Polish	1	Sentenced in W. Germany to 5.5 yrs.
1981	S	Poland	W. Germany	Polish	12	Sentenced in W. Germany to terms ranging from 1 to 4 yrs.

(continued)

Table 5.1 *(Continued)*

Year	Result	Flight Originating From	Hijackers Apprehended in	Registry	No. of Persons Apprehended	Disposition of Case
1981	U	Yugoslavia	Cyprus	Yugoslavian	3	Turned over to Yugoslavian officials in Cyprus; sentenced in Yugoslavia to terms of 8, 5 and 3.5 yrs.
1981	U	India	Pakistan	Indian	7	Charges pending in Pakistan
1982	S	U.S.	Cuba	U.S.	1	Reportedly sentenced in Cuba to 12 yrs.
1982	S	Tanzania	England	Tanzanian	5	Charges pending in England
1982	S	U.S.	Cuba	U.S.	3	Reportedly sentenced in Cuba to 20 yrs.
1982	S	Poland	W. Germany	Polish	8	Sentenced in W. Germany to terms ranging from 2.5 to 4 yrs.
1982	S	U.S.	Cuba	U.S.	2	Reportedly sentenced in Cuba to 15 yrs.
1982	S	USSR	Turkey	USSR	3	Charges pending in Turkey
1982	S	Bulgaria	Austria	Bulgarian	2	Sentenced by Austrian court to 2 yrs. and 1 yr. (1 yr. sentence suspended)

Total prosecutions 38
Total sentenced 35

S = Successful
U = Unsuccessful

Table 5.2 International Rendition of Hijackers, 1977–1981

Extraditions

Year	Requesting State	Requested State	No. of Persons	Result
1977	USSR	Sweden	1	Denied; prosecuted; sentenced to 4 yrs.
1977	Bulgaria	Yugoslavia	1	Disposition unknown
1978	Netherlands	Spain	1	Granted
Total:			3	
Granted:			1	

Deportations

Year	Flight Originating from	Where Apprehended	Deported to	No. of Persons	Registry
1977	U.S.	Ireland	U.S.	1	U.S.
1977	Japan	Japan	U.S.	1	U.S.
1977	Chile	Peru	Cuba	4	Chile
1977	Lebanon	Kuwait	Lebanon	1	Lebanese
1979	U.S.	Mexico	U.S.	1	U.S.
Total:				5	

Exclusions

Year	Excluded from	Returned to	No. of Persons
1977	England	U.S.	1
1977	Finland	USSR	2
1978	Switzerland	U.S.	1
1979	India	Bangladesh	1
1979	Cyprus	Libya	1
1980	Cuba	U.S.	2
1981	Cyprus	Yugloslavia	3
Total:			7

Expulsions

Year	Flight Originating from	Where Apprehended	Expelled to	
1979	Nicaragua	Costa Rica	Panama	
Total:				1

Total Dispositions*	48
Prosecution	38
Exclusion	8
Deportation	5
Extradition	1
Expulsion	1
Sentenced	35

*Including prosecutions, Table 5.1

Table 5.3 Persons Involved in the Seventy-two Hijackings of U.S.-Registered Aircraft, 1977-1982

Convictions	40
Domestic 34	
aForeign 6	
Acquittals	2
Mental institution	5
Dismissed or prosecution declined	10
Killed/suicide	4
Pending	11
bFugitives	31
Total	103

aThose prosecutions were in Cuba.
bListed officially as fugitives; all were involved in hijackings to Cuba and were taken into custody by Cuban officials; dispositions unknown.
Average sentence: 24 yrs.
Range of sentence: 4 mos. + probation to life.
Average sentence when air piracy or kidnapping charge: 30 yrs. (2 life sentences)

tion, and 73 to the Montreal Convention.[12] Moreover, there have been some significant additions to the lists of parties to the Hague and Montreal conventions since 1977. These include, for example, Afghanistan (Hague Convention), Libya (Hague and Montreal conventions) and Syria (Hague and Montreal conventions).

To be sure a state's status as a party does not ensure that it will fulfill its obligations under a convention—as demonstrated by Uganda (Entebbe) and Afghanistan (Pakistani Airline hijacking). But such a status at a minimum gives other states parties standing to complain of a violation and, even in the absence of an enforcement convention, may greatly enhance the pressure states parties can bring to bear against the violator to fulfill its obligations.

At this writing a bizarre incident involving civilian aviation, complex questions of international law, and high political drama has been concluded, at least as far as the civilian aircraft is concerned. According to newspaper reports,[13] on July 5, 1984, Umaru Dikko, former Nigerian Transport Minister under the recently deposed government of President Sheku Shagari, was dragged from his home near London's Hyde Park and found in a drugged stupor in a crate that was to be loaded on a Nigerian cargo plane. Although the crate was addressed to the Nigerian Foreign Ministry in Lagos, the Nigerian government denied any involvement in the incident. Upon detention of the cargo plane, the Nigerian government detained a British Caledonia passenger jet in Lagos. Scotland Yard arrested four men believed involved in the attempt to kidnap Dikko, who is wanted by the new Nigerian military government for alleged corruption while in

Table 5.4   Summary of Hijackings, 1977–1982

		Successful					
		U.S.		To Cuba		General Aviation Flights	
Year	Total Worldwide	%	No.	%	No.	%	No.
1977	32	6	(18.75)	0		2	(6.25)
1978	31	13	(41.93)	4	(12.9)	6	(19.35)
1979	27	13	(48.15)	6	(22.22)	4	(14.81)
1980	41	22	(53.66)	21	(51.21)	3	(7.31)
1981	32	8	(25)	6	(18.75)	3	(9.38)
1982	32	10	(31.25)	5	(15.63)	2	(6.25)
Totals	195	72	(36.92)	42	(21.54)	20	(10.26)

	Unsuccessful or Incomplete			
Year	Worldwide	U.S.	Worldwide %	U.S. %
1977	16	6	50	100
1978	21	11	68	85
1979	13	7	48	54
1980	19	9	46	41
1981	17	6	53	75
1982	16	6	50	60
Total	102	45	52	63

Successful: Controls flight and reaches destination or objective.
Unsuccessful: Fails to control flight.
Incomplete: Apprehended or killed during hijacking or as result of "Hot Pursuit".

office. Two of the four men arrested were reportedly Israeli mercenaries; the other two were Nigerians. None had any apparent official governmental status. The Israeli Embassy denied any involvement or previous knowledge of the incident.

Before opening two suspicious crates, the British Foreign Office had to determine whether, under the 1961 Vienna Convention on Diplomatic Relations, the crate might be covered by the principle of diplomatic inviolability, like the diplomatic pouch. The Foreign Office reportedly decided that the crates were not immune because they did not "bear visible external markings of their character" and because there was no diplomatic courier with the crates with "an official document indicating his status." After this decision, an order was given to open the crates, but not before an official of the Nigerian Embassy was called to witness the action, as required by the Vienna Convention.

The standoff between the British and Nigerian governments ended on July 7, when the Nigerian Airway Boeing 707 was allowed to depart four hours after police released all but four of the seventeen people questioned in connection with the abduction. The British plane left Lagos a few hours later.

Also at this writing the Indian government is seeking the return from Pakistan of nine Sikh hijackers who commandeered an Indian Airlines jet with about 250 people aboard and demanded that it fly to Pakistan.[14] India and Pakistan have no extradition treaty, but both countries are parties to the Hague Convention, which can be used as an extradition treaty. India is also seeking the hijackers' return as part of an agreement on prisoner exchanges. Pakistan negotiated the safe release and return of the plane and its passengers, but has reportedly indicated it will try the hijackers in Pakistan rather than return them to India. If it does so in accord with its usual criminal law procedures, Pakistan will have fulfilled its obligations under the Hague Convention.

What is one to conclude from this record as to the effectiveness of current law and procedures designed to apprehend, prosecute, and punish those who engage in threats and attacks against civil aviation? In this writer's opinion, although the data are incomplete and inconclusive, they support the thesis that, in the face of manifest and manifold difficulties, the current system is working with a substantial measure of efficiency. A large number of countries have now become parties to the civil aviation conventions. Operating within the framework of these conventions, these states have rendered a substantial number of hijackers back to requesting states or have opted to submit them to prosecution, with the result often being the imposition of a severe penalty. It appears that a large number of states have concluded that it is in their common interest to punish, and thus discourage, attacks on civil aviation. A recent indication of this attitude is Cuba's imposition of severe penalties against hijackers of airplanes from the United States to Cuba, despite the continued, if not intensified, tension between the United States and Cuba and the lack of any formal treaty arrangement between the two countries covering the crime.

To be sure, the record could and should be improved. Recommendations to this end are presented in the next chapter.

Other Manifestations of Terrorist Activity

As indicated in the introduction to this chapter, data on the apprehension, prosecution and punishment of those who commit terrorist acts other than attacks on civil aviation are extremely sparse, and not collected, analyzed, or disseminated in any systematic fashion. Accordingly, one can gain only fleeting impressions of state practice in these other areas. One area that does stand out, however, especially recently, is attacks on diplomats and diplomatic facilities, and it is to this subject we turn in the first subsection.

ATTACKS ON DIPLOMATS AND DIPLOMATIC FACILITIES

As noted in a recent report of the Office for Combating Terrorism, U.S. Department of State,[15] diplomats have become the major target of international terrorists. The figures tell the tale. In 1975, 30 percent of all international terrorist attacks were directed against diplomats; in 1980 the number increased to 54 percent and has remained at that level for the last three years. Diplomatic casualties reached a high in 1981, dropped only slightly in 1982, and with the April 18th bombing of the United States Embassy in Beirut, the department was predicting that the number would be up again in 1983.

Assassination attempts against diplomats jumped sharply in the mid-1970s and reached their peak at 29 in 1980; in 1982, the number was 21. The large number of assassinations and attempted assassinations in 1979, 1980, and 1981 was due in large part to the campaign of Armenian terrorists against Turkish diplomats and terrorist activities associated with the Iran-Iraq war.

Diplomatic kidnappings and hostage-barricade operations have also increased in number in recent years. In 1980, the number for these types of events almost doubled from the year before, and the high point was reached in 1981. After declining in 1982, the number was up again in the first four months of 1983.

Bombings have long been the preferred method of attack against diplomats, as well as against other targets, since they involve little rsk of capture, and explosives are relatively easy to obtain. Most of these bombings have not caused extensive damage, although there are exceptions that result in the loss of life and the destruction of diplomatic facilities. One of the most destructive attacks of this nature was the April 1983 bombing of the United States Embassy in Lebanon, which destroyed an entire wing of the building and killed more than 60 people, including 17 American citizens.

As of January 1, 1984, there were 61 states parties to the Convention on the Prevention and Punishment of Crimes Against Internationally Protected Persons, Including Diplomatic Agents (the New York Convention).[16] Compared with the number of states parties to the Civil Aviation Conventions, this is not an impressive figure. One of the reasons there are not more states parties may be the resolution by which the United Nations General Assembly adopted the convention,[17] which some, incorrectly in this writer's view, interpret as *authorizing* attacks on diplomats or diplomatic facilities if such attacks are committed in a struggle for self-determination against "colonialism, alien domination, foreign occupation, racial discrimination, and *apartheid*."[18] Nonetheless, despite the relative paucity of states parties to the convention, those who attack diplomats or diplomatic facilities have often been prosecuted and subjected to severe penalties.

In the United States, attacks against diplomats and other internationally protected persons have been vigorously prosecuted, and these efforts have resulted in a number of convictions.[19] The constitutionality of the laws implementing the New York Convention has been upheld by the courts, and the courts have interpreted and applied their terms expansively.[20]

Even more so than in the case of terrorist attacks against civil aviation, the data regarding state practice towards the apprehension, prosecution, and punishment of those who attack diplomats or diplomatic premises are sparse. However, states have enacted legislation implementing their obligations under the New York Convention and have utilized such legislation for purposes of prosecution.[21] The extent to which the New York Convention has been utilized as the basis for rendition of alleged offenders is less clear. Nor is it clear the extent to which methods of rendition other than extradition have been utilized in the state of refuge in lien of a prosecution by the state for attacks on diplomats. The data are simply not available at this writing.

A POTPOURRI

When one moves from attacks on civil aviation, or on diplomats and diplomatic facilities, to other manifestations of terrorism such as hostage taking, attacks on international business persons, bombings and other attacks against civilians, and so forth, one finds no systematic collection whatsoever of information regarding the apprehension, prosecution, and punishment of the perpetrators of these acts. Neither the government nor private agencies specializing in combating international terrorism have been much interested in collecting this kind of data.

Accordingly, one is forced to rely on accounts from newspapers, magazines, court reports, and other information sources.[22] Even these sources more often than not focus their attention on the terrorist incident itself, the perpetrators of it, and the victim, rather than on prosecution and punishment. Nonetheless, even if on an unsystematic and largely unscientific basis, one can gain certain impressions from these sources that may be relevant to efforts to combat international terrorism.

One largely unanswered question is the extent to which terrorism is increasing in intensity and destructive effect and poses a major problem for future world stability. At a recent conference, Lord Chalfont, an eminent British writer and scholar, stated:

> Since 1968, when official statistics were first compiled, there have been 8,000 major terrorist incidents; over 8,000 people have been wounded, and nearly 4,000 killed; and, even more significantly the graph of terrorism has risen and is still rising. According to U.S. government figures, the number of attacks rose from under 200 in 1968 to 800 in 1983; the number of attacks which

caused death or injury rose from about 25 in 1968 to over 200 in 1980, and is still rising.[23]

Similarly, at the same conference, U.S. Secretary of State George P. Schultz reported:

> The distressing fact is that over these past five years terrorism has increased. More people were killed or injured by international terrorists last year than in any year since governments began keeping records. In 1983, there were more than 500 such attacks, of which more than 200 were against the United States.[24]

On the other hand, Australian scholar Grant Wardlaw has pointed out:

> A recent report by the United States Central Intelligence Agency (CIA) illustrates that even compilation of statistics of international terrorism are fraught with danger. Since 1968, the CIA has kept computerized records on international terrorism . . . These records are used to compile an annual report on international terrorism. The 1980 report was interesting in that it completely revised many of the figures published in previous years. The agency said that its previous data had been too dependent on "U.S. sources" and that it is now satisfied that its records are "complete and current." The report also listed several new categories, including "threats" and "hoaxes" which had not been listed in previous reports. Thus, whereas the 1979 report said that there had been 3,336 incidents of international terrorism between 1968 and 1979, with a peak of 413 in 1976, the 1980 report claimed that there were 6,714 incidents between 1968 and 1980, with 760 in 1979. According to the CIA there were 587 deaths due to international terrorism in 1979 and 642 in 1980. The fact that an agency with the resources of the CIA can conclude that at a particular point in time that many of its previously published statistics were underestimates makes it difficult to have confidence in the accuracy of their figures. How do they know they have obtained all the relevant data now — or, more particularly, how can we be assured that they have? It is because of these uncertainties that many students of terrorism are wary of making precise quantitative analyses of trends in terrorism.[25]

Secretary Schultz himself recognized that there has been some progress made by way of *prevention* of terrorist activiy:

> If we remain firm, we can look ahead to a time when terrorism will cease to be a major factor in world affairs. But we must face the challenge with realism, determination, and strength of will. Not so long ago we faced a rash of political kidnappings and embassy takeovers. These problems seemed insurmountable. Yet, through increased security, the willingness of governments to resist terrorist demands and to use force when appropriate, such incidents have become rare. In recent years, we have also seen a decline in the number of air-

line hijackings—once a problem that seemed to fill our newspapers daily. Tougher security measures and closer international cooperation have clearly had their effect.[26]

As to the future, Yonah Alexander has suggested the following reasons to support the proposition that terrorism is likely to increase both at home and abroad:

1. Terrorism has proved successful again and again in attracting publicity, disrupting government and business, and in causing significant death and destruction.
2. Arms, explosives, supplies and financing are readily available.
3. International connections among states, especially between the Soviet Union and the Third World can and do greatly facilitate terrorist activities.
4. Terrorist groups are continually able to exploit conditions of social unrest, including East-West issues, such as deployment of Euromissiles.
5. International controls, coordination and cooperation geared towards combating international terrorism remain weak.
6. Ninety percent of the terrorist groups in the world are Marxist, and pro-Marxist sympathies (which the Soviet Union and its surrogates support) have increasingly grown the world over.[27]

Regardless of the present situation concerning the incidence and magnitude of terrorism, or the likely future trend in this area, the apprehension, prosecution, and punishment of international terrorists will be an important factor in combatting international terrorism. With respect to the current situation, the impression one gains from a reading of the limited data available is that states are becoming increasingly willing to prosecute and punish international terrorists or to render them up to another country that will. It appears that Italy, for example, through a combination of effective police work (as in the Dozier kidnapping), harsh sentences for terrorism, and incentives (in the form of reduced sentences for informants), has achieved a significant decline in terrorism, although there is some question about the durability of this decline.[28]

At the same time, Italy has consistently given preferential treatment to Arab terrorists, probably because of its heavy dependence on oil from Arab states. Only with respect to terrorist activity targeting Libyan exiles in Italy has the government cracked down on Arab terrorists. And even here the approach has been to deport alleged offenders rather than to subject them to trial and possible imprisonment in Italy. In an apparent tacit exchange for this treatment, Arab terrorists have avoided attacking Italian targets.[29]

The Federal Republic of Germany is well known, if not notorious, for its hard line against terrorists. A number of critics have charged that Germany has gone too far in its approach and has undermined fundamental liberties in doing so.[30]

In any event, there have been exceptions to this hardline approach. For example, Germany has on several occasions been a safe-haven for anti-Yugoslav Croatian emigrees.[31] In several instances, German courts declined to permit the extradition of such emigrees charged with criminal behavior in Yugoslavia. By way of retaliation, Yugoslavia declined a German request for the extradition of Germans sought for the alleged commission of terrorist crimes. Also, prior to the murder at Munich in 1972 of the Israeli Olympic athletes, Germany tended to adopt a "soft line" approach in negotiations with terrorists in hostage situations.

Germany has been active, and indeed a leader, in cooperative efforts between European police and security forces designed to combat terrorism.[32] They have also been active in seeking, with mixed success, the extradition or other rendition of German terrorists from other countries. One of the more interesting cases in this connection was the 1978 deportation by Bulgaria of Baader-Meinhoff members to the Federal Republic of Germany. Bulgaria's motivation in doing so is unclear. Reportedly, Bulgaria agreed to deport the alleged terrorists in exchange for the FRG's agreement not to prosecute the Bulgarians operating in Germany as spies.[33]

Another unusual dilemma arose in 1980 when the German government arrested two Iraqi citizens on suspicion of attempting to assassinate Kurdish students in Berlin. Although the German government initially announced they would prosecute the Iraqis, they were instead deported to Iraq, allegedly because of strong pressure from the Iraq government.[34] Finally, German intelligence agents reportedly entered into a secret agreement in 1979 with the Palestine Liberation Organization whereby the PLO agreed not to conduct terrorist operations on German soil.[35]

As discussed earlier in this study, the French practice regarding apprehension, prosecution, and punishment of international terrorists has varied considerably over the last few years. French practice with respect to extradition, in particular, has appeared to reflect the political currents of the moment. At the same time, the record indicates that French law enforcement officials have been willing to utilize exclusion and deportation methods in situations where formal extradition proceedings might be unsuccessful as a method of return.[36] On the other hand, the Mitterand government has announced that it is reconsidering extradition treaties with Turkey, Italy, and Spain on the ground that extradition of alleged offenders to these countries might be inconsistent with fundamental human rights. Also it has strongly emphasized adherence to the principle of asylum for political offenders.[37] At this writing the likely future practice of the French government is simply unclear.

In its efforts to combat Basque terrorism, Spain has consistently been frustrated by France's refusal to grant its requests for extradition.[38] For its part, in June 1974, Spain denied a Swedish extradition request for nine Croatian airplane hijackers on the ground that the Swedish request did not contain a strict promise not to charge the persons sought with an offense they had allegedly committed prior to and allegedly unconnected with the extradition request. The nine were, however, tried and convicted in Spain.[39]

Some recent experience in Colombia demonstrates continued adherence of Latin American states to the doctrine of political asylum. In June 1982, the Supreme Court of Colombia ruled that Leandro Barraci, who had been charged with being a member of the Red Brigades and who was involved with the murder of Aldo Moro, could not be extradited to Italy because the acts with which he was charged constituted political offenses.[40]

Notes

1. See, e.g., U.S. Department of State, *Patterns of International Terrorism: 1981* (July 1982).
2. See, e.g., *FBI Analysis of Terrorist Incidents in the United States*, 1982.
3. See, e.g., *Major Accomplishments of the FBI Terrorism Program*, 1982.
4. Evans, "The Apprehension and Prosecution of Offenders: Some Current Problems," in A. E. Evans and J. F. Murphy, eds., *Legal Aspects of International Terrorism* (1978), p. 493.
5. U.S. Department of State, *Terrorist Skyjackings* (July 1982).
6. These data are taken from documents kindly supplied this writer by the Office of Civil Aviation Security, Federal Aviation Administration, Department of Transportation.
7. Evans, "The Apprehension and Prosecution of Offenders: Some Current Problems," supra note 4, at 494–95.
8. These data are taken from documents kindly supplied this writer by the Office of Civil Aviation Security Federal Aviation Administration, Department of Transportation. I wish to express appreciation for the assistance rendered by Marguerite Trossevin, a third-year student at the Villanova Law School, in compiling these data and preparing the tables that follow in the text.
9. Evans, "Aircraft and Aviation Facilities," in A. E. Evans and J. F. Murphy, eds., *Legal Aspects of International Terrorism*, (1978), pp. 3, 16.
10. See U.S. Department of Transportation, Federal Aviation Administration, Office of Civil Aviation Security, *Legal Status of Hijackers: Summarization* (Jan. 1, 1983).
11. See U.S. Department of State, *Treaties in Force*, 209–11 (Jan. 1, 1984).
12. Evans, "Aircraft and Aviation Facilities," supra note 9, at 20.
13. *Philadelphia Inquirer*, July 8, 1984, at 7-A.
14. Id.
15. U.S. Department of State, *Terrorist Incidents Involving Diplomats*, 1 (Aug. 1983).
16. See *Treaties in Force*, supra, note 11, at 297.
17. U.N. DOC. A/9407, at 63, 64 (1973).
18. See Murphy, "Protected Persons and Diplomatic Facilities," in A. E. Evans and J. F. Murphy, eds., *Legal Aspects of International Terrorism* (1978), pp. 277, 311–12.
19. See, e.g., United States v. Garcia, 456 F. Supp. 1358 (D. P.R. 1978), aff'd 622 F.2d 12 (1st Cir. 1980); United States v. Layton, 509 F. Supp. 212 (N.D. Cal.), aff'd 645 F.2d 681 (9th Cir. 1981).
20. United States v. Garcia, 622 F.2d 12 (1st Cir. 1980). See also United States v. Layton, 645 F.2d 681 (9th Cir. 1981).
21. See Report of the U.N. Secretary General, *Consideration of Effective Measures to Enhance the Protection, Security and Safety of Diplomatic and Consular Missions and Representatives*, U.N. Doc. A/38/379, Sept. 20, 1983.
22. Perhaps the most helpful of these other sources of information was a series of studies on the impact of government behavior on the frequency, type, and targets of terrorist group

activity undertaken by the consulting firm Defense Systems, Inc., located in McLean, Virginia. The firm very kindly permitted this writer to have access to the data they had compiled in the course of their study, and, where applicable, reference will be made in the following footnotes to the data so supplied.

23. Statement of Lord Chalfont at the opening session of the Jonathan Institute's Second Conference on International Terrorism, June 24, 1984, Washington, D.C., at 3-4.

24. Address by the Honorable George P. Schultz to the Jonathan Institute's Second Conference on International Terrorism, at 1.

25. G. Wardlaw, *Political Terrorism: Theory, Tactics and Counter-Measures,* 50-51 (1982).

26. Address by the Honorable George P. Schultz, supra note 24, at 17.

27. Alexander, "The Spiraling Price of Modern Terrorism," *American Jewish Congress Monthly*, 22-23 (Jan./Feb. 1984).

28. Based on data supplied this writer by Defense Systems, Inc.

29. Id.

30. See, e.g., Weiss, "Joe McCarthy is Alive and Well and Living in West Germany: Terror and Counter-Terror in the Federal Republic," *New York University Journal of International Law and Politics*, 9 (1976): 61.

31. Based on data supplied this writer by Defense Systems, Inc.

32. Id.
33. Id.
34. Id.
35. Id.
36. Id.
37. Id.
38. Id.
39. Id.
40. Id.

CHAPTER 6

Conclusions and Recommendations

In this final chapter, we attempt to reach conclusions regarding the problem areas previously discussed and to come up with recommendations for change in law and policy designed to improve the record of the world community in apprehending, prosecuting, and punishing international terrorists. As we do so, our primary goal should be borne in mind: The effective punishment of those who commit terrorist acts in accordance with law and procedure that fully protects their fundamental human rights.

Some of the problems in *apprehending* international terrorists have been briefly noted in Chapter 4. These have been explored extensively in other forums and will not be considered further here.[1] Rather, we shall proceed in the following fashion. First, we shall examine methods of rendition—extradition, exclusion, and deportation—both as they are employed in United States law and practice and in terms of international initiatives. Next, we shall turn to prosecution and punishment and the protection of fundamental human rights, including international judicial assistance in criminal matters. Last, we shall conclude with a brief look at the thorny problem of safe-haven states.

Although it is not the method most often chosen by states to return terrorists to the place where they committed their crimes, extradition is the method of return envisaged by the antiterrorist conventions and, most important, the method designed to protect the fundamental rights of an accused. Accordingly, the need for reforms in extradition law and practice is especially urgent, and we turn to some possibilities in the next section.

Extradition — United States Law and Practice

CONCLUSIONS

In Chapter 2 we considered in some detail bills pending before Congress that would reform United States federal extradition statutes. At this writing, for a variety of political reasons, none of these bills is likely to become law. This is unfortunate for, as demonstrated fully in Chapter 2, current legislation, at a minimum, is badly in need of streamlining to ensure that extradition is not so time-consuming and burdensome a process as to be dysfunctional to efforts to combat international terrorism. In addition, there is a need to come to grips with the problem of the political offense exception.

To be sure, one should not exaggerate the political offense problem as a barrier to extradition of terrorists under United States law and practice. In only four cases out of hundreds—*Mackin, McMullen, Quinn,* and *Doherty*— has the political offense exception barred the extradition of a person accused of a terrorist act. Political rhetoric to the contrary notwithstanding, the United States has not become a "haven" for international terrorists because of the approach of its courts to the political offense exception; the problem should be kept in proper perspective. Nonetheless, the problem exists, and potentially could become more acute; it, therefore, should be resolved if possible.

The primary approach taken by the United States so far to resolve the problem has been to insert clauses in its bilateral extradition treaties expressly narrowing the scope of the political offense exception to exclude attacks against a head of state or head of government or their families and any "offense with respect to which the Contracting Parties have the obligation to prosecute or to grant extradition by reason of a multilateral international agreement."[2] Or, alternatively, a clause in a bilateral extradition treaty will reserve the decision on the political offense exception to the executive branch of the contracting parties, which, in the case of the United States, will presumably be inclined to define the scope of a political offense exception narrowly. This latter approach raises the issue, discussed in chapter 2, of whether the decision on the political offense exception should be reserved to the courts. In any event, revision of the 90-plus extradition treaties of the United States is a time-consuming and laborious process as compared to dealing with the problem through legislation.

Two other aspects of United States extradition law relevant to international terrorists should be briefly noted. The first is that the United States will not extradite an individual to a requesting state unless it has a bilateral extradition treaty with that government.[3] Some other nations extradite as a matter of comity, often on the basis of their national legislation. The second is that United States extradition law, unlike its immigration law, does not expressly recognize a bar to extradition even if the accused would be persecuted in the requesting state on account of race, religion, or political opinion. Rather, under the rule of non-inquiry adopted by United States courts, the executive branch may, in its sole discretion, decide whether to extradite under such circumstances.[4]

RECOMMENDATIONS

The first recommendation is self-evident. Congress should complete its work on revising extradition laws. General revision of United States extradition law would contribute to the effort to combat international terrorism because it would make the process more efficient and less time-consuming and hence encourage law enforcement officials to make greater use of it. With specific reference to international terrorism, the following reforms should be given highest priority.

First and foremost, United States extradition legislation should be revised so as to exclude from the political offense exception acts of international terrorism. This might be accomplished either by a modest or minimal approach or by a more ambitious or maximal initiative.

The modest approach would be simply to exclude from the political offense exception attacks on heads of state or heads of government and any offense covered by an antiterrorist convention to which the United States is a party—thus tracking the exclusion contained in the recently concluded United States-Costa Rica Extradition Treaty.[5]

The more ambitious approach, the one favored by this writer, would be to define international terrorism in the legislation and explicitly exclude it from the political offense exception. It is important to note that a definition of international terrorism already appears in United States federal legislation. The Foreign Intelligence Surveillance Act defines acts of international terrorism as "activities that involve violent acts or acts dangerous to human life that are a violation of the criminal laws of the United States or of any State, or that would be a criminal violation if committed within the jurisdiction of the United States or any State."[6] In order to distinguish international terrorism from a great variety of other crimes, the definition goes on to require that these acts "appear to be intended (A) to intimidate or coerce a civilian population; (B) to influence the policy of a government by intimidation or coercion; or (C) to affect the conduct of government by assassination or kidnapping."[7]

To ensure an international dimension, the definition requires that the acts "occur totally outside the United States or transcend national boundaries in terms of the means by which they are accomplished, the persons they appear intended to coerce or intimidate, or the locale in which their perpetrators operate or seek asylum."[8] This part of the definition is also intended to cover acts of "transnational terrorism," such as the kidnapping of a foreign official in the United States by a foreign terrorist group in order to affect the conduct of the foreign official's government. It would also include a United States terrorist group's placement of a bomb in a foreign airplane or its receipt of directions or substantial support from a foreign government or terrorist group.

Other definitions are possible, of course, such as the one currently employed by the United States government in gathering information about international terrorism or the working definition of the International Law Association's Committee on International Terrorism. But whatever the definition finally agreed upon, the time has come to give explicit guidance to United States courts to ensure that international terrorists do not escape extradition because of the political offense exception.

Express exclusion of international terrorism from the political offense exception would be a major step toward increasing the efficiency of United States extradition law and practice and thereby enhance the probability that international terrorists would be subject to prosecution and punishment for their crimes. The question also arises, however, whether current United States law and practice fully protects the fundamental rights of a person accused of terrorism who is the subject of an extradition request. As to this question, this writer agrees with Professors Barbara Ann Banoff and Christopher H. Pyle that it does not, because an accused can be extradited to a country where he would be persecuted on account of his race, religion, or political opinion under the rule of non-inquiry adopted by the United States judiciary.[9] Most United States extradition treaties provide that extradition shall be denied if the true purpose of the request is to persecute the person sought for his political opinion, race, religion, or nationality. However, although compatibility with treaty requirements is one of the issues within their jurisdiction, the courts have consistently declined to inquire into the foreign government's motives for seeking extradition, or the fairness of its judicial system.

On the face of it, this is an anomaly, since deportation of an accused to such a country is expressly prohibited by United States law.[10] Moreover, it is highly debatable whether the judiciary should defer to the executive branch in cases involving claims of political persecution upon return. This writer agrees with Banoff and Pyle that in a democratic society, "the judicial system is the proper institution to protect individuals from the political vagaries of governments."[11]

On October 4, 1983, the House Judiciary Committee adopted an amendment to H.R. 3347, offered by Congressman Robert W. Kastenmeier, which would abolish the rule of non-inquiry and substitute an affirmative obligation to inquire into the treatment a returned accused would be likely to receive.[12] Specifically, the amendment would prohibit extradition of an accused if that "person has established by a preponderance of the evidence that he: (i) is being sought for prosecution or punishment because of such person's race, religion, sex, nationality, membership in a particular social group or political opinion; (ii) would, as a result of extradition, be subject to fundamental unfairness."[13]

As pointed out by Professors Banoff and Pyle, the United Kingdom has adopted a statute that mandates the type of inquiry envisaged by the Kastenmeier Amendment.[14] The Fugitive Offenders Act of 1967, which applies to intra-Commonwealth extradition, provides that no one shall be returned to a requesting country if it appears that he may be "prejudiced at his trial or punished, detained or restricted in his personal liberty by reason of his race, religion, nationality or political opinions."[15]

Banoff and Pyle have also suggested a helpful list of factors that a United States court might consider in making an inquiry under the Kastenmeier Amendment as to whether a requesting state's judicial process is suspect:

(1) The investigation of the crime was conducted by a different law enforcement branch than that which normally conducts such criminal investigations;

(2) The decision to prosecute deviates from normal prosecutorial discretion in that country, as evidenced, for example, by the resurrection of an unenforced law;

(3) A political leader has intervened in the decision to investigate or prosecute;

(4) The defendant will be tried in a different court than that used for ordinary criminals;

(5) The defendant will be tried by a form of revolutionary tribunal;

(6) The requesting state maintains separate penal or interrogation facilities for political prisoners, and the requesting government intends to interrogate or confine the defendant in such facilities;

(7) The defendant, or a group with which he or she has been actively associated, is politically controversial or has been the target of systematic discrimination;

(8) The defendant has been the target of political surveillance, covert harassment or official criticism either in the requesting state or in the United States;

(9) The defendant has actively opposed the policies or the legitimacy of the requesting state's government, either while resident there or elsewhere, in a manner which has provoked reprisals from that government against others similarly situated;

(10) The issues involved in the case are so controversial that it is doubtful the accused could receive a fair trial or, if convicted, a fair sentence; or

(11) The requesting state cannot guarantee the physical safety of the accused if he or she is returned.[16]

Last, Banoff and Pyle point out that under the Kastenmeier Amendment the choice would not necessarily be between unconditional extradition and no extradition. Current law grants a magistrate who has to decide a political offense case only two alternatives: to grant or deny the extradition request.[17] Banoff and Pyle propose that the option of conditional orders of extradition be available to the decision maker as they are in non-political cases. They suggest, for example, that if "the defendant has shown that he or she may be tried in a special court, confined under special conditions or interrogated with unusual techniques, the grant of extradition may be conditioned on the requesting state's agreement to use its ordinary courts, prisons or investigative methods."[18]

Extradition — International Initiatives

CONCLUSIONS AND RECOMMENDATIONS

At the international level the United States should continue to pursue the negotiation or renegotiation of bilateral extradition treaties incorporating provisions that, at a minimum, would follow the United States–Costa Rica extradition model in excluding attacks on heads of state and government as well as offenses covered by the antiterrorist conventions from the political offense exception and that ideally would define international terrorism so as to exclude terrorist acts generally. To be sure, this process will be time-consuming and involve difficult negotiations, but it is worth the effort.

On a global basis, the time may have come when the United States and like-minded countries should consider a major new initiative in the United Nations. This writer fully recognizes and appreciates the difficulties the United States faces in that Organization. Nonetheless, as noted more fully elsewhere,[19] the United Nations has taken some constructive steps toward combating terrorism, and there may be opportunities for further initiatives.

Specifically, the report of the International Law Association's Committee on international terrorism, discussed in Chapter 2, might serve as a basis for a draft resolution — to be introduced in the General Assembly by a country other than the United States — that would incorporate a definition of international terrorism along the lines of that of the committee, or some other suitable source, as well as some of the principles and statements of law proposed by the committee. The world community has probably gone about as far as it can with the piecemeal approach to combating terrorism; the time may now have come to consider a more comprehensive step.

Ideally, this step might take the form of a draft convention. But the political climate does not appear to have evolved to the point where the drafting of a comprehensive convention on terrorism would be anything more than an exercise in futility.

The same may not be true, however, for a draft resolution, and it should be kept in mind that, in United Nations practice, a General Assembly resolution often serves as a precursor to a convention on the same subject. In any event, even if the General Assembly should fail to adopt such a resolution, a debate on the principles and statements of law expressed in it would be beneficial. As John Norton Moore has said, we are today faced with a "struggle for law."[20] The International Law Association committee's report elaborates principles and statements of law that all states of goodwill should adopt in the effort to apprehend, prosecute, and punish international terrorists. Even if they were not to receive the United Nations imprimatur of approval in the form of a General Assembly resolution, a debate on these principles and statements of law might induce many states to follow them in their practice outside of the organization, for example, by incorporating them in national legislation and in bilateral or multilateral treaties. At a minimum the educational value of a debate in the General Assembly would be considerable.

Exclusion and Deportation

CONCLUSIONS AND RECOMMENDATIONS

As noted previously in this study, exclusion and deportation have been favored, at least by many countries other than the United States, over extradition as the method of rendition for international terrorists. This perhaps would change, in some measure, if extradition were made more efficient along the lines suggested earlier. A shift from the use of exclusion and deportation to extradition would be greatly facilitated by the adoption of national legislation along the lines of the Austrian Law on Extradition and Mutual Assistance in Criminal Matters, which explicitly prohibits utilizing deportation as a method for circumventing extradition—a prohibition which applies even prior to the filing of a formal request for extradition in any case where extradition to a foreign state would appear warranted.[21]

It is clear, however, that exclusion and deportation will continue to be heavily utilized as methods of rendition of international terrorists. The problem with the use of exclusion and deportation as methods of rendition is that while they are highly efficient in returning an accused to the place where he allegedly committed a crime—that is why they are utilized in lieu of extradition—this efficiency is often achieved at the cost of violating the fundamental rights of an accused. To effect a better balance between efficiency and due process, exclusion and deportation should not be used as methods of rendition when to do so would result in an accused being tried for a political offense (defined in such a way as to exclude acts of terrorism) or being prosecuted on account of his race, religion, or political opinion.

Since exclusion and deportation are basically domestic civil procedures not designed for the purpose of cooperation in furthering the international criminal justice system, it is doubtful whether the reforms suggested in the previous paragraph could be effected through international agreement. To be sure, as we have seen, the convention and protocol relating to the status of refugees are applicable, albeit indirectly, to use of exclusion and deportation as methods of rendition. But it is doubtful that states would be willing to go beyond the convention and protocol and conclude an international agreement explicitly putting limits on their use of exclusion and deportation as methods of rendition. Rather, these reforms are likely to take place, if at all, at the domestic level through the enactment or revision of national legislation.

This is not to say, however, that nothing can be done by way of international initiative to encourage such domestic reforms. For example, the use of exclusion and deportation as methods of rendition could be discussed in the United Nations. Member states could be encouraged, by General Assembly resolution, to report on their national law and practice regarding exclusion and deportation. Model legislation to serve as a guide to member states might be drafted and incorporated in a General Assembly resolution. This approach would utilize education and example as an inducement to action in place of the creation of an international legal obligation in treaty form.

Prosecution, Punishment, and the Protection of Fundamental Human Rights

CONCLUSIONS

As noted in various places in this study, the goal of the world community, which methods of rendition are designed to further, is the prosecution and punishment of persons accused of terrorism in a manner consistent with their fundamental human rights. This is demonstrated most emphatically by the "extradite or prosecute" provision commonly contained in the antiterrorist conventions.

It must be remembered, however, that the extradite or prosecute formula, except in the case of the European Convention on the Suppression of Terrorism, applies only to a limited number of crimes and not to "terrorism" per se. Hence, in many, perhaps most, instances, the requested country is under no obligation to submit an accused terrorist to prosecution if it declines to extradite him.

To be sure, this conventional wisdom has been challenged by the International Law Assoociation's Committee on International Terrorism, which has proposed as a statement of law that "States must try or extradite (aut judicare, aut dedere) persons accused of acts of international terrorism." One may doubt whether this is a statement of the *lex lata*; but in any event, assuming *arguendo* that current law is as suggested by the committee, few states are in a position to carry out their obligation. That is, while states parties to the applicable conventions have enacted legislation giving their courts jurisdiction to try persons accused, for example, of attacks against civil aviation or internationally protected persons, few have statutes on the books investing their courts with jurisdiction over international terrorism. In other words, even if international terrorism has or might become a crime subject to universal jurisdiction, states must take the additional step in their national laws to permit the exercise of such jurisdiction.

RECOMMENDATIONS

Although this writer has been skeptical about the desirability of a federal statute that would permit United States courts to exercise jurisdiction over acts of international terrorism, he has come around to the view that such a statute is both desirable and needed. The arguments in favor of such a statute have recently been presented in cogent fashion by Professor Paust.[22] A basic point Paust makes is that, in the absence of such a statute, a gap exists in United States law that prevents the United States from fulfilling its responsibilities under international law to prosecute international terrorists.

In response to Paust's proposal, Professor Brent Smith has raised some troubling issues.[23] He argues that terrorism should not be defined as a distinct form of criminal activity for two basic reasons. First, "terrorism" is inherently fraught with conceptual difficulties in tying the definition of the offense to the motives or ideology of the group. Second, as demonstrated by the experience in several foreign countries, the enactment of legislation defining terrorism as a separate crime may give rise to numerous opportunities for governmental overreaction and a consequent threat to civil liberties.

These are real concerns. It should be noted, however, that the proposal is to create a crime of *international* terrorism under United States law. There is no need, and it would be dangerous, to create a crime of "terrorism" applicable to criminal acts with no international dimension. In this situation, the danger of governmental abuse could be considerable, as Smith illustrates in his discussion of "terrorist threat" statutes found in some states in the United States.[24] As to purely domestic terrorism, Smith is right in suggesting that existing legislation, both federal and state, is an adequate response.

In respect to international terrorism, however, the situation is different. International terrorism, unlike domestic terrorism, poses a threat to peaceful and prosperous relations among member states of the world community. Indeed, it is this element that most strongly supports the proposition that international terrorism is a threat to the entire world community and should be subject to the universality principle of criminal jurisdiction.

Moreover, as Paust has pointed out in response to Smith's second argument, there are ways to avoid overly broad "terrorism-specific" statutes.[25] Specifically, Paust stresses the need for an express reference to the political purpose of the perpetrator and a terror outcome that is actually threatened or occurs. This would distinguish international terrorism, Paust suggests, from, for example, a mere aggravated assault. He suggests further that a "descriptive definitional approach will incorporate salient characteristics and allow one to focus on strategies of terrorism."[26] Paust would define terrorism as "any intentional use of violence or a threat of violence against an instrumental target in order to communicate to a primary target a threat of future violence so as to coerce the primary target through intense fear or anxiety in connection with a demanded political outcome."[27]

On balance the case in favor of federal legislation creating a crime of international terrorism seems convincing. Such legislation might also serve as a model for other countries to follow and might as well be a useful supplement to provisions in bilateral and multilateral extradition agreements defining international terrorism for purposes of exclusion from the political offense exception.

If such legislation were enacted in the United States and abroad, the next step might be to revise extradition treaties to incorporate an "extradite or prosecute" requirement applicable to international terrorism. This has been proposed by other commentators as well.[28]

International Judicial Assistance in Criminal Matters

CONCLUSIONS AND RECOMMENDATIONS

If the United States and other countries were to adopt legislation giving their courts jurisdiction over acts of international terrorism, as suggested in the previous section, the need for reform regarding international judicial assistance in criminal matters would become particularly acute. Some of the problems and possible remedies in this area have been discussed in chapter 4, and that discussion will not be repeated here. For present purposes, it suffices to point to the primary problem of particular relevance to the prosecution of international terrorism: the obligation under mutual judicial assistance treaties on the requested country to assist the requesting country in obtaining evidence for use in criminal proceedings in the requesting country does not apply if the offense charged is political. Moreover, as we have seen in chapter 4, few mutual judicial assistance treaties the United States is currently a party to expressly exclude acts of terrorism from the political offense exception.

This should be changed, and as a matter of high priority. The process of revision would basically parallel that suggested above in the section on extradition. Ideally, mutual judicial assistance treaties should contain provisions defining and expressly excluding acts of international terrorism from the political offense exception.

A Brief Word on the Problem of Safe-Haven States

CONCLUSIONS AND RECOMMENDATIONS

One of the more disturbing developments of the 1980s is the rise of state-sponsored terrorism or, as it is sometimes called, wars of assassination. This development was marked initially by the 1978 umbrella murder of Georgi Markov by Bulgarian agents in London, and more recently by such events as the North Korean-sponsored bombing in Rangoon of South Korean political leaders; the attempt on the life of the Pope; the attack on Jordanian envoys on three continents by Syrian agents around the time of the Arafat-Hussein talks of 1983; the assassination of Bachar Gemayel, again by Syrian agents; the Kuwaiti bombings by Iranian agents; and the shooting of a British policewoman from the Libyian embassy in London. Such actions amount to interstate armed conflict and should be subject to the constraints placed on the unilateral use of force by states under articles 2(4) and 51 of the United Nations Charter, as well as other applicable norms of international law.

Merely providing safe-haven to international terrorists raises more complex issues, because it is not clear that, by doing so, the state has violated any international obligation — at least in the absence of the safe-haven state being a party to an applicable international convention. In issuing the Bonn Declaration, the summit countries, in effect, claimed that states offering safe-haven to aircraft hijackers were violating an international obligation owed to the world community — regardless of whether they were parties to the civil aviation conventions — and claimed the right to apply sanctions against such states. At this writing this claim has not been extended at the interstate level beyond aircraft hijacking.

However, the report of the ILA Committee on International Terrorism does claim, as a matter of law, that states are obligated to extradite or prosecute those who commit acts of international terrorism. Should this claim gain wide acceptance — either through the claim and counter-claim process of customary international law, or in the form of treaties — the case in favor of applying economic sanctions against safe-haven states would be strengthened.

An urgent issue on the world community's agenda is how to respond to state-sponsored terrorism. To the extent that states engaged in wars of assassinations and safe-haven states are one and the same, the problem of offering safe-haven becomes submerged in the larger issue.

Even with respect to those states that do not go beyond offering safe-haven to international terrorists, the need for meaningful multilateral economic sanctions is becoming more acute. This writer has been skeptical regarding the usefulness of economic sanctions against safe-haven states.[29] As time passes, however, and the diplomatic process fails to induce such states to refrain from undermining international efforts to apprehend and prosecute international terrorists, the need for more coercive measures becomes apparent. At a minimum, as suggested by Professor Lillich and others,[30] where standing exists, safe-haven states should be subject to international claims challenging such practices as a violation of international law.

Notes

1. See, e.g., Kerstetter, "Practical Problems of Law Enforcement," in A. E. Evans and J. F. Murphy, eds., *Legal Aspects of International Terrorism* (1978), p. 535.
2. Article 4(2)(b), Extradition Treaty Between the Government of the United States of America and the Government of the Republic of Costa Rica, ratified by the United States on Aug. 17, 1984, according to the Treaty Affairs Office of the U.S. Department of State.
3. See Bassiouni, "Remarks to the Panel on International Procedures for the Apprehension and Rendition of Offenders," *Proceedings of the American Society of International Law* (1980): 274, 277.
4. See In re Ezeta, 62 F. 972 (N.D. Cal. 1894); Jimenez v. Aristequita, 311 F. 2d 547 (5th Cir. 1962); Garcia-Guillern v. United States, 540 F. 2d 1189 (5th Cir. 1962). But cf. In re Mylonas, 187 F. Supp. 716 (N.D. Ala. 1960).
5. See supra note 2.
6. 50 U.S.C. §1801(c)(1) (Supp. III 1979).
7. Id., §1801(c)(2).
8. Id., §1801(c)(3).
9. See the cases cited in note 4, supra, and associated text.
10. 8 U.S.C. §1253 (1970 and Supp. 1984).
11. Banoff and Pyle, " 'To Surrender Political Offenders': The Political Exception to Extradition in United States Law," *New York University Journal of International Law and Politics 16* (1984): 169, 210.
12. Id., at 199.
13. Id.
14. Id., at 202.
15. Fugitive Offenders Act, 1967, ch. 68, §4(1).
16. Banoff and Pyle, supra, note 11 at 202-3.
17. Id., at 205.
18. Id., at 206.
19. J. F. Murphy, *The United Nations and the Control of International Violence* (1983), p. 175-202.
20. John Norton Moore, Walter L. Brown Professor of Law at the University of Virginia, has made this point at a number of conferences in which the author has participated.
21. See E. Palmer, *The Austrian Law on Extradition and Mutual Assistance in Criminal Matters* (1983), p. 32.
22. Paust, "Federal Jurisdiction Over Extraterritorial Acts of Terrorism and Nonimmunity for Foreign Violators of International Law Under the FSIA and the Act of State Doctrine," *Virginia Journal of International Law* 23 (1983): 191.
23. Smith, "Antiterrorism Legislation in the United States: Problems and Implications," *Terrorism: An International Journal,* 7.2 (1984): 213.
24. See also "Validity and Construction of 'Terroristic Threat' Statutes," 58 ALR 3rd 533 (1972).
25. Paust, "Terrorism and 'Terrorism-Specific' Statutes," *Terrorism: An International Journal* 7.2 (1984): 212.
26. Id.

27. Paust, "Terrorism and the International Law of War," *Military Law Review* 64 (1974): 1.
28. See C. Van den Wijngaert, *The Political Offense Exception to Extradition* (1980).
29. See Murphy, "State Self Help and Problems of Public International Law,'" in A. E. Evans and J. F. Murphy, eds., *Legal Aspects of International Terrorism* (1978), p. 553, 565.
30. Lillich and Paxman, "State Responsibility for Injuries to Aliens Occasioned by Terrorist Activities," *American University Law Review* 26 (1977): 217. See also Rubin, "Current Legal Approaches to International Terrorism," in H. H. Han, ed., *Terrorism, Political Violence and World Order* (1984), p. 433.

Index

Abduction of alleged criminals, 89–93
Abu Eain v. Adams, 51, 70
Afghanistan, 20–21
"Aircraft and Aviation Facilities" (Evans), 30, 34n
Alexander, Yonah, 120, 123n
American Bar Association, 66–67
American Declaration of the Rights and Duties of Man, 42
Anti-Hijacking Act of 1974, 21–23
"Antiterrorism Legislation in the United States" (Smith), 132, 135n
Apprehension, 107–23
"The Apprehension and Prosecution of Offenders" (Evans), 101–2, 103n
ARHG. *See* Austrian Law on Extradition and Mutual Assistance in Criminal Matters
Armed conflict, law of, 11, 66
Artukovic v. Boyle, 50
Asylum, 40–41, 88, 89, 121
Australia, 88
Austria
   extradition legislation in, 55–56, 74–77, 130
   and judicial assistance, 100–101
   prosecution in, 75–76
   refugees and deportation in, 88
Austrian Extradition Act, 55–56
Austrian Law on Extradition and Mutual Assistance in Criminal Matters (ARHG), 74–77, 130

Aut dedere, aut judicare, principle of, 14, 36, 59
Aviation, attacks against, 108–16 (*see also* Hijackers and hijacking)

Banoff, Barbara Ann, 127–29, 135n
Bassiouni, M. C., 1, 5n
International Extradition: United States Law and Practice, 83–84, 90, 92, 93n
Baxter, Richard, 3, 5n
Belgian Extradition Act of 1883, 47
Belgium, refugees and deportation in, 88
Bonn Declaration, 19–21, 134
Brazil, refugees and political offense theory in, 88–89
Britain. *See* United Kingdom
Bulgaria, 121
Bulut, Faik, 90

Canada, 99
Castione case, 47–48
Chalfont, Lord, 118–19
Chicago Convention, 18–19
Chile, 27
Colombia, 122
Commonwealth nations, 37, 71
Comprehensive Crime Control Act of 1983, 63–64, 65–66, 68–69
Constitution, U.S., law and treaty in, 79n

Convention Relating to the Status of Refugees, 82–83, 131
Conventions, counterterrorist, 9–35
  against hijacking, 109–15
  bilateral, 16–17
  global, 9–11, 62
  regional, 11–16
  United States and, 68–69
Conventions, extradition
  regional, 37–42
  See also Extradition; Treaties, extradition
Cordero case, 92
Costa Rica, 43, 126
Council of Europe, 38
Court decisions, foreign, on the extradition of political offenders, 47–49, 53–56
Court decisions, U.S.
  concerning diplomats, 24–27
  on deportation, 85–86, 87
  on evidence obtained abroad, 96–97
  on the extradition of political offenders, 49–53
  on hijacking, 22–23
  on illegal methods of rendition, 90–92
Croissant, Klaus, case of, 53–54
Cuba
  hijackings to, 108, 116
  and the United States–Cuba Memorandum, 16–17

Death penalty, 74, 77
Denmark, counterterrorist legislation in, 30
Deportation, 81–89, 130–31
  Austrian law on, 76
  for hijacking, 109
  and human rights, 83–84
  in international law, 82–84
  legal standards for, 82
  in U.S. law, 85–88
"Deportation and the Refugee" (Griffith), 87–88, 93n
Dikko, Umaro, 115–16
Diplomats
  attacks on, 116–18
  global conventions concerning, 10
  International Law Association on, 60
  international legislation concerning, 30

  U.S. court decisions concerning, 24–27
  U.S. legislation concerning, 23–24
Doherty, Joseph Patrick Thomas, case of, 52–53
Dublin Agreement, 15–16

Eichman, Adolf, Israeli abduction of, 89–90
England. *See* United Kingdom
Europe, 38
European Convention on Extradition, 38
European Convention on Human Rights, 84
European Convention on the Suppression of Terrorism, 13–15
European Human Rights Convention, 101
Evans, Alona, 30, 34n, 81, 93n, 101–2, 103n
Exclusion, 81–89, 130–31
  for hijacking, 109
  and human rights, 83–84
  in international law, 82–84
  legal standards for, 82
  in U.S. law, 85–88
Extradition, 36–80
  ad hoc, 72–73
  in Austria law, 55–56, 74–77
  in British law, 70–74
  among Commonwealth nations, 71
  Cuba and, 16
  in the Dublin Agreement, 15
  in the European Convention on the Suppression of Terrorism, 13–15
  in global conventions, 10, 62
  for hijacking, 109
  legal standards for, 69, 72–73, 76–77, 81
  limitations on, 44
  in the OAS Convention, 12
  offenses subject to, 43–44
  Republic of Ireland and, 71–72
  in Swiss law, 55
  in the United States–Cuba Memorandum, 16
  in U.S. law, 62–66, 67–69, 124–29
  See also Conventions, extradition; Treaties, extradition
Extradition Act of 1984, 64–65, 67
  Kastenmeier Amendment to, 127, 128

Federal Aviation Administration (FAA), 22
Federal Bureau of Investigation (FBI), 108
"Federal Jurisdiction Over Extraterritorial Acts of Terrorism" (Paust), 132–33, 135n
Foreign Intelligence Surveillance Act, 126
France
  asylum in, 89
  and the Bonn Declaration, 20
  and the European Convention on the Suppression of Terrorism, 15
  extradition court decisions in, 53–54
  and terrorists, 121
Fugitive Offenders Act of 1967, 128

Germany, Federal Republic of
  asylum in, 89
  and the Bonn Declaration, 20
  and terrorists, 120–21
Gonzales case, 50
Griffith, Dean, 87–88, 93n
Grotius, Hugo, 46

Hague Convention, 109–15
Haitians, 85
Hijackers and hijacking
  conventions covering, 109–15
  court decisions concerning, 22–23
  by Cubans, 108
  harboring of, 17–19
  incidents of, 108, 110–12 (table), 114 (table)
  International Law Association on, 60
  legislation concerning, 21–23
  prosecution and punishment for, 109, 116
  rendition for, 109, 113–14 (table)
  sanctions against, 16–21
Holder-Kerkow case, 53
Hostage taking
  international conventions concerning, 31–32, 32n
  U.S. legislation concerning, 29
Human rights
  exclusion and deportation and, 83–84
  extradition and, 127–29
  illegal rendition and, 92–93
  in the Inter-American Convention on Extradition, 42
  prosecution, punishment, and 131–33

"Ideologically Motivated Offenses" (Bassiouni), 1, 5n
In re Castione, 47–48
In re Gonzales, 50
In re Latelier v. Republic of Chile, 27
In re Mackin, 51
In re McMullen, 50–51, 86
In re Meunier, 47–48
India, 116
Inter-American Convention on Extradition, 39–42
International Civil Aviation Organization (ICAO), 17–19
International Convention Against the Taking of Hostages, 31–32, 32n
"International Exchange of Information in Criminal Cases" (Tigar and Doyle), 95–96, 102n
International Extradition: United States Law and Practice (Bassiouni), 83–84, 90, 82, 93n
International law concerning exclusion and deportation, 82–84
International Law Association resolution on terrorism, 56–62, 129–30, 131, 134
Interpol, 96
Ireland, Republic of
  and the European Convention on the Suppression of Terrorism, 14–15
  extradition arrangements with U.K., 71–72
Irregular Extradition (Warbrick), 84, 93n
Israel
  and the case of Faik Bulut, 90
  counterterrorist legislation in, 31
  and the kidnapping of Adolf Eichmann, 89–90
Italy
  asylum in, 89
  judicial assistance treaty with United States, 97–98
  and terrorists, 120

Jimenez v. Aristeguieta, et al., 49–50
Judicial assistance, 11, 133–34
  Austrian law on, 100–101
  international, 95–103

political offense exception and, 98
U.S. law on, 96–100
Jurisdiction
  in Austrian criminal law, 75
  in the New York Convention, 26–27

Kastenmeier Amendment to the Extradition Act of 1984, 127, 128
"Ker-Frisbie" doctrine, 90, 93
Kolczynski case, 48

Latelier case, 27
Layton case, 26–27
Lechoco case, 24–26
Legislation, foreign
  on asylum, 89
  counterterrorist, 30–31
  on exclusion and deportation 88–89, 94n
  on extradition, 55–56, 70–74, 128, 130
  on judicial assistance, 100–101
  on refugees, 88–89
Legislation, U.S.
  concerning exclusion and deportation, 85–88
  on extradition, 124–29
  on judicial assistance, 96–100
Lira case, 91
Lockheed Aircraft Corporation, 99
Lujan case, 91

Mackin v. Grant, 51
McMullen case, 50–51, 86
Meunier case, 47–48
Mexico
  counterterrorist legislation in, 31
  judicial assistance treaty with U.S., 99
Mitterand, François, 15
Montevideo Convention, 115
Montreal Convention, 115

Netherlands, exclusion and deportation in, 89, 94n
New York Convention, 10–11, 24, 26–27, 117–18
Nigeria, 115–16

Nordic Treaty of 1962, 37
Nuclear materials, theft of, 27–29

OAS Convention, 11–13, 33
"Obtaining People and Evidence from Abroad" (Evans), 81, 93n
Office for Combating Terrorism, 107, 117

Paust, "Federal Jurisdiction Over Extraterritorial Acts of Terrorism," 132–33, 135n
Piperno case, 54
Political offense exception in ad hoc extradition arrangements, 73–74
  American Bar Association on, 66–67
  in the European Convention on Extradition, 38
  in the European Convention on the Suppression of Terrorism, 13–15, 33n
  history of, 46–47
  in the Inter-American Convention on Extradition, 40
  International Law Association on, 58
  and judicial assistance, 98
  military targets and, 70
  rationales for, 45–46
  in regional counterterrorist conventions, 12–13
  and terrorism, 45–77
  U.S. law on, 62–66, 67–69, 125–27
The Political Offense Exception to Extradition (Wijngaert), 45–46, 47, 49, 50, 53, 54–55, 78n
Political offense, theories of, 45, 47–56, 87–88, 88–89
Political Terrorism: Theory, Tactics and Counter-Measures (Wardlaw), 229, 123n
Prosecution, 107–23
  for attacks against diplomats, 118
  in Austrian law, 75–76
  in the European Convention for the Suppression of Terrorism, 14
  in global conventions, 10–11, 62
  for hijacking, 109, 116
  and human rights, 131–33
  in the Inter-American Convention on Extradition, 41–42

in the International Convention Against the Taking of Hostages, 32n
in the OAS Convention, 13
and political asylum, 41
in the United States–Cuba Memorandum, 16
Protocol Relating to the Status of Refugees, 82–83, 131
Punishment, 107–23
for hijacking, 109, 116
and human rights, 131–33

Quinn, William Joseph, 70
case of, 51–52

Reciprocity, 75
Refugees, 82–83, 87, 88
Regina v. Governor of Brixton Prison, ex parte Kolczynski, 48
Regina v. Governor of Brixton Prison, ex parte Schtraks, 48–49
Regina v. Governor of Pentonville Prison, ex parte Tzu-Tsai Cheng, 49
Rendition
formal and informal methods of, 36
illegal methods of, 89–93
informal methods of, 81–89

Sabotage, against aircraft, 109
Save-haven states, 17–19, 134
Scandinavian states, 37
Scheme Relating to the Rendition of Fugitive Offenders, 37
Schtraks case, 48–49
Schultz, George P., 119–20
A Skeptical Look at the Concept of Terrorism (Baxter), 3, 5n
Smith, Brent, 132, 135n
Soviet Union, 19
Spain, 121–22
Specialty, doctrine of
in extradition treaties, 43
in the Inter-American Convention on Extradition, 40
"The Spiraling Price of Modern Terrorism" (Alexander), 120, 123n
Swiss Extradition Act, 55
Switzerland, 55, 97

Terrorism
apprehension, prosecution and punishment for, 107–23
definition of, 1, 3–5, 57, 126–27, 129, 132–33
increasing intensity of, 118–20
information on, 107–8
and military targets, 70
political offense exception and, 45–56, 56–77
state support for, 59
Tigar, Michael
"International Exchange of Information in Criminal Cases," 95–96, 102n
Tokyo Convention, 109–15
Toscanino case, 90–91
Treaties, extradition
Austrian bilateral, 74–75
bilateral, 42–45
U.K. bilateral, 80
U.S. bilateral, 67–68, 125, 127, 129
Turkey, 98–99
Tzu-Tsai Cheng case, 49
See also Conventions, extradition; Extradition

United Kingdom
bilateral treaties of, 80n
and the Bonn Declaration, 20
extradition arrangements with Ireland, 71–72
extradition court decisions in, 47–49
extradition legislation in, 70–74
United Kingdom/Swiss proposal, 18
United Nations, 129
Convention Against the Taking of Hostages, 11
United States
counterterrorist court decisions in, 22–23, 24–27
counterterrorist legislation in, 21–24, 27–29
extradition court decisions in, 49–53
extradition legislation in, 62–66, 67–69
extradition treaties of, 43–45
on the harboring of hijackers, 17–18
and judicial assistance, 96–100
United States ex rel. Lujan v. Gengler, 91
United States v. Cordero, 92

United States v. Layton, 26–27
United States v. Lechoco, 24–26, 34n
United States v. Lira, 91
United States v. Toscanino, 90–91
United States v. Valot, 91–92
United States–Cuba Memorandum, 16–17
Universal Declaration of Human Rights, 83–84
University principle, 62, 75
Unlawful seizure, 89–93

Valot case, 91–92

Warbrick, Colin, *Irregular Extradition*, 84, 93n
Wardlaw, Grant, *Political Terrorism: Theory, Tactics and Counter-Measures*, 119, 123n
Wijingaert, Christine Van den, *The Political Offense Exception to Extradition*, 53, 45–46, 47, 49, 50, 54–55, 78n